Primates of the World

Jean-Jacques Petter and François Desbordes

Translated by Robert Martin

PRINCETON UNIVERSITY PRESS   Princeton and Oxford

Primates of the World

AN ILLUSTRATED GUIDE

Published by Princeton University Press, 41 William Street, Princeton, New Jersey 08540

In the United Kingdom: Princeton University Press, 6 Oxford Street, Woodstock, Oxfordshire OX20 1TW

press.princeton.edu

Jacket art © François Desbordes

ISBN 978-0-691-15695-8

Library of Congress Control Number: 2013930446

British Library Cataloging-in-Publication Data is available

This book has been composed in Garamond Premier Pro and Myriad Pro

Printed on acid-free paper.

Printed in China

10 9 8 7 6 5 4 3 2 1

Contents

The Beginning of an Adventure

Ever since the time of the first civilizations, nonhuman primates and people have oc-cupied overlapping habitats, and it is easy to imagine how important these first contacts were for our ancestors' philosophical reflections.

Long ago, adopting a quasi-scientific view, some people accordingly regarded pri-mates as transformed humans. Others, by contrast, respected them as distinct be-ings, seen either as bearers of sacred properties or, conversely, as diabolical creatures.

A Rapid Tour around the World

In Egypt under the pharaohs, science and religion were still incompletely separated. Priests saw the *Papio hamadryas* living around them as "brother baboons" guarding their temples. In fact, the Egyptian god Thoth was a complex deity combining qualities of monkeys and those of other wild animal species living in rice paddies next to temples, all able to sound the alarm if thieves were skulking nearby.

At first, baboons represented a local god in the Nile delta who guarded sacred sites. The associated cult then spread through middle Egypt. Even-tually, this god was assimilated by the Greeks into Hermes Trismegistus, the deity measuring and interpreting time, the messenger of the gods. One conse-quence of this deification was that many animals were mummified after death to honor them.

Ancient Egyptians used traits of an ibis or a Hamadryas Baboon (*Papio hamadryas*) to represent their god Thoth.

In northern India, monkeys of a different kind known as "sacred langurs" (*Semnopithecus entellus*) were regarded as manifestations of the god Hanuman. According to legend, Hanuman and his army helped the prince Rama (reincarnation of the god Vishnu) to find his fiancée, Sita, after a giant had carried her off. Sacred langurs had free access to dwellings and wandered freely in the streets. They were, and still are, greatly venerated in this region, where they occupy certain temples. Despite the inconvenience of their presence, local human populations still protect them.

The Indian "sacred langur" (*Semnopithecus entellus*), regarded as a descendant of the god Hanuman, is venerated by Hindu populations.

Like baboons in ancient Egypt, Japanese Macaques (*Macaca fuscata*) are protected, as are various other macaque species in different parts of the world. However, some societies have linked macaques to ancient humans that had been punished by Allah, doubtless because of their postures and behavior.

Around the world, people have held this relatively high level of respect for and accompanying primitive beliefs about the local primates. Despite their competition with people, primates have acquired a privileged status in comparison with other members of the local fauna.

Protection has also existed for monkeys and apes in Africa and Asia, for some species in the forests of South and Central America, and even for certain large-bodied lemurs in Madagascar, such as the Indri (*Indri indri*), which is notable for maintaining a vertical body position while leaping. Even today, Indris are often still regarded as human ancestors that preferred to remain in the forest. Their territorial vocalizations and the long, modulated howls that they utter from time to time in the forest are interpreted as cries of desolation, expressing their lonely existence.

Primates and Humankind

The Japanese Macaque (*Macaca fuscata*), a universal figure in local myths and fables, is respected and protected in Japan.

In regions where the natural fauna included no nonhuman primates, the first apes and monkeys imported were predominantly seen as caricatures of humans. Only the primates that looked the most human-like were thought to have a passable allure. The human model was so powerful in people's imaginations that everything about our closest relatives seemed deplorable. Their capacity for imitation and intelligence were seen only in a negative light. Almost everything to do with them was considered grotesque.

Even the eminent naturalist Alfred Edmund Brehm wrote, some 150 years ago: "In no other order in the mammalian class does one find such a lack of harmony as in primates. . . . Primates have nothing that could give them any claim to beauty, and the advantages that they have over other animals are merely apparent. One might perhaps think that having four hands makes them superior to humans, who only have two. But that is not the case. The sages of Antiquity already considered the hand to be the most important organ, the physical attribute that makes us human. But the hand of a monkey or ape is just an imperfect imitation of the perfect human hand."

More recently, Jean Henri Fabre, the famous French entomologist—who was admired for his skillful studies of insects, his intelligence, his precision, and his capacity for critical thought—came up with the following statement to refute the "transmutationism" of his friend Darwin: "If we are told in all seriousness that: 'In the present state of science it has been convincingly shown that humans descended from some scarcely enhanced macaque'... we need to take a close look at aptitudes. What differences, what a chasm of separation.... At the very least, one might expect to be shown an animal somewhere making a tool, multiplying its force and dexterity, and mastering fire, that fundamental key to progress. Mastery of tools and fire! These two capacities, however simple they may be, characterize a human being far more than the numbers of his vertebrae or molar teeth."

In making this rather simplistic judgment, relating everything to modern, "civilized" humans, Fabre ignored the importance of the multiple adaptations of the primates, which seemed to constitute a homogeneous group but were very poorly known in his time. Above all, their evolution seemed to have favored the behavioral capacities of arboreal locomotion, leaping, and running. In fact, behavioral capacities have been also favored in human evolution. These capacities have become exceptional, thanks to marked expansion of the human brain, bestowing a degree of liberty that is unique in the animal kingdom.

Fabre's generalizations were faulty and are somewhat surprising to read today. In his time, the behavioral patterns of different primate species were poorly known. Since then considerable progress has been made, notably through painstaking analyses of their behavior based on field studies conducted in the habitats where they live.

Modern ethology, the science of animal behavior, aided by the powerful techniques of photography, video, and sound recording as adjuncts to sophisticated methods of observation, has now revealed that Common Chimpanzees (*Pan troglodytes*) and Bonobos (*Pan paniscus*) know how to make tools. They use these "multipliers of force and dexterity," in Fabre's formulation, very skillfully to acquire food. Admittedly, they do not use fire, but modern humans doubtless took a considerable time to master it themselves.

Our generation is privileged in comparison with those that will follow, because we are still able to witness, before it is destroyed, what is

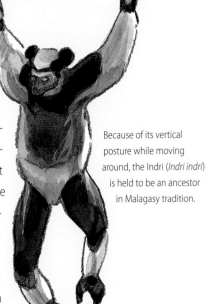

Because of its vertical posture while moving around, the Indri (*Indri indri*) is held to be an ancestor in Malagasy tradition.

Detail from the decoration of La Grande Singerie (the large monkey house) at the Château de Chantilly in France. The caricatures in this mural, painted in the eighteenth century, have been attributed to the French painter Christophe Huet.

left of a natural world that helps us to understand a little about our own origins. If we do not protect our monkey and ape "brothers," it will no longer be possible to observe that, according to many criteria, they were barely more primitive than we are. If we do not take into account the kaleidoscopic succession of primates, it is possible to imagine the "creation" of human beings with no past, opening up a wide arena for unbridled imagination. It is a pity that somebody with Fabre's undoubted talents was unable to grasp this. Despite their language differences, Darwin himself had admired Fabre's pioneering studies of instinct in insects and noted his analytical prowess. Regrettably, the friendly relationship that developed between these two men was too short-lived to permit Fabre to acquire a better understanding of the evolution of primates and of human nature.

In the meantime, primates have been well studied, at first in captivity and then under natural conditions as well. Gradually, research in zoos and laboratories, supplemented by expeditions to the habitats in which primates live, has generated a substantial mass of information on all aspects of this group. Notably, meeting Fabre's demand in his anti-Darwinian reflections, knowledge has accumulated regarding their behavior under natural conditions, their social life, and their use of tools and gestural language. In parallel, detailed information has been collected on the anatomy and physiology of various species, their relationships, their reproduction, their sensory capacities, and all the other aspects required for complex syntheses.

However, all of this accumulated knowledge lacked a historical extension into the past, toward our distant ancestors. If viewed with caution, such a perspective is provided by paleontologists. Their findings provide an introduction to our origins, starting at the time when dinosaurs were replaced by the predecessors of modern mammals.

In Search of Our Origins

The principal characters of primates (recognized as the "first" among mammals by the Swedish naturalist Carolus Linnaeus) are: expansion of the brain, an omnivorous dentition—without any particular specialization—and, in most cases, forelimbs ending in hands with flat nails on their fingers. In fact, the group cannot be defined by any character that it alone possesses. At the outset, systematic divisions are intuitive, and detailed studies then yield more precise definitions that allow us to separate one group from another. And this is true at all levels in the hierarchy of living organisms. Recent classifications have drawn upon studies of resemblances in the chemical structures of proteins and, increasingly, on comparisons of DNA sequences.

Nonhuman primates now occupy tropical forests (in so far as they still exist) almost throughout the world, with the exception of Australia and New Guinea. However, fossils belonging to this group have been found in Europe, Asia, North America, and Argentina at much higher latitudes than their modern relatives occur.

Anatomical and Physiological Acquisitions of Mammals

Starting more than 200 million years ago, and continuing throughout the Mesozoic era, small-bodied mammals lived side-by-side with reptiles, progressively acquiring the characters that define modern mammals. Their predecessors, the mammal-like reptiles, had appeared at the end of the Carboniferous period and flourished during the Permian and Triassic periods. They were linked to the mammal lineage by a distinctive character separating them from other reptiles: the presence of a temporal fenestra, a single aperture on the skull, opening just behind the orbit.

A group of reptiles known as cynodonts, which gave rise to the first family identified as mammals (morganucodontids, known from teeth, incomplete skulls, and some skeletal material), documents a major transformation from the primitive reptilian state to the mammalian condition: the development of a new joint for the lower jaw. The bones that formed the primitive reptilian joint (articular and quadrate) were gradually reduced to become two additional ossicles in the middle ear (malleus and incus).

Reptiles are generally unable to react to variations in temperature. They have to be warmed by the sun before foraging for food and then digesting it. They can attain impressive sizes only if they live in isolated regions with a warm climate, such as the island of Komodo (Indonesia), where the famous "dragons" can still be found. Moreover, reptiles are exposed to fluctuations in the external environment because of their egg-laying mode of reproduction.

Compared to reptiles, the ancestors of mammals had relatively large brains. Direct control of body temperature was developed, favoring greater functional constancy in the sensory apparatus and higher efficiency in hunting prey. A certain degree of independence from external conditions was acquired quite rapidly.

In the realm of reproduction, development of offspring was eventually able to proceed either in a pouch (still in a fetal condition), as in marsupials, or through acquisition of a placenta inside the mother's body.

The First Mammals Appear

As a general rule, the first representatives of any group of animals to appear (the first members of any given order) are small in size.

During the Cretaceous period, differentiation of small-bodied insectivores and the first hoofed mammals can already be seen. The insectivores gave rise to the first primates, which rapidly found protection in the forests. Little by little, this early mammalian fauna diversified, with body size gradually increasing, while the last dinosaurs became extinct. Remains of these early mammals have been found, but they are rare. These fossils exhibit the typical architecture of the skull, direct articulation of the dentary constituting the lower jaw with the skull, a large brain cavity, the presence of three ossicles in the middle ear, and differentiation of the teeth into incisors, canines, premolars, and molars, with their number and form characterizing individual species. The upper and lower teeth interlock (occlude) in close contact, generating wear patterns that differ distinctively among species. The anatomical configuration of the anterior and posterior limb bones permits locomotion with the body raised above the ground, departing from the creeping gait of reptiles and permitting greater efficiency and reduced energy expenditure.

The evolutionary diversification of mammals is essentially restricted to the Tertiary period. The characters that we recognize for this group—warm-bloodedness, possession of hair, production of milk to nourish offspring—are obviously almost impossible to recognize in the precious fossil remains of their Mesozoic predecessors. To construct our vision of the past and to define the origin of primates, we must refer both to paleontology and to our understanding of extant species.

The Precursors of Mammals

From Dinosaurs to Primates

The long evolutionary history of the primates begins soon after the emergence of the early placental mammals, at a time when the large-bodied reptiles were on their way to extinction. Their existence is documented by fossil remains of small-bodied creatures that fed mainly on insects and other invertebrates.

Dinosaurs dominated Earth during the Mesozoic era, and the groups of small-bodied mammals were able to diversify only toward the end of their reign. These mammals were discreet, nocturnal creatures that were able to survive the upheaval that seemingly marked the end of the Cretaceous. Many hypotheses have been proposed to explain the extinction of the dinosaurs, including impact of a giant meteorite generating climatic perturbation, climatic cooling due to a worldwide resurgence of volcanism and shrinking of the oceans, and extinction provoked by new predators. Hypotheses of abrupt destruction have been countered by proposals of gradual extinction extending over millions of years, in either case leaving a major ecological vacuum. Unlike typical dinosaurs, small mammals were able to move around rapidly among the branches of trees, and this represented a huge advantage.

The First Primates

Understanding of the lives of these emerging primate species and their differentiation had to await the nineteenth century and the ideas of Georges Cuvier, Jean-Baptiste Lamarck, Charles Darwin, and the biologists that followed them, along with studies conducted by the first geneticists.

Demographic factors surely played an important part in evolution. In fact, phases of population isolation occurred repeatedly. In a theoretical unlimited population in which individuals reproduce freely, all with an equivalent probability of producing descendants, the frequency of any given gene is stable. By contrast, the more a population is subject to limitation, the more the frequencies of genes are modified over successive generations. Heterozygotes possessing alternative expressions of a given character tend to disappear, leaving the way open for homozygotes with only one possible expression of a given character and hence subject to strong selection. This is why whenever an environment leads to "isolates" subject to reproductive constraints, populations develop along different trajectories.

Two main groups of Eocene primates have been recognized:

- Omomyiforms, which are linked to tarsiers, nocturnal inhabitants of Southeast Asia. Their remains include fossils resembling modern tarsiers, which are distinguished from other small-bodied primates by their extreme adaptation for leaping. Omomyiforms were once a flourishing, greatly diversified assemblage that has been interpreted as the ancestral source from which the human lineage evolved. Representatives were already present in Asia 50 million years ago.
- Adapiforms, which are known from numerous fossils found in France in the phosphorite deposits (natural accumulations of phosphate of lime) of Quercy, in North America and, more recently, in Egypt, in the Fayum deposits.

In the Eocene numerous species of these early primates existed, diverging in different evolutionary directions, although many are known only from teeth. It is hoped that continued paleontological excavations and investigations will resolve as yet unanswered questions about them.

Around 50 million years ago, these two groups of primates occupied forests in certain regions of the world. Presumably, they were already well adapted both anatomically and with respect to sensory capacities for life in the trees, and expansion of the brain was already under way. But the route between those early primates and ourselves is a long one, and of course we cannot trace an exact itinerary.

Specialists have endlessly discussed the position of tarsiers in relation to other primates. When did tarsiers diverge from the lineage leading to higher primates, the monkeys and apes? Did this occur before or after the divergence of strepsirrhines (lemurs and lorises)?

Explanations of how primitive African primates reached Madagascar or South America are still in the realm of supposition. Ethologists—scientists who study animal behavior—have only a minor role to play in such reconstructions of past events. They can only imagine, on the basis of their own studies, the lives of animals described by paleontologists.

Fossils of "true" Old World simians with thirty-two teeth, dating back thirty to forty million years, have been discovered at the site of Fayum (sixty miles from Cairo), alongside forms with thirty-six teeth that show characters very reminiscent of the characters of New World monkeys (platyrrhines) of South and Central America. The first group includes small-bodied forms (e.g., *Oligopithecus*), large-bodied forms (e.g. *Aegyptopithecus*), and some that are in between. The origins of the main types of modern higher primates are already represented. The family containing species with thirty-six teeth has been named Parapithecidae. Paleontological research conducted in South America, at a site in Bolivia, yielded dental remains almost as old as Fayum fossils.

The Expansion of Primates

From the very beginning, the expansion of primates involved Europe and North America, which together formed an immense landmass. Numerous adapiforms, related to those found in Paris and Quercy, have been discovered in North America. Much more recently, similar primates have been found in Madagascar, but only in Quaternary deposits, thus raising the question of their origin.

A similar question arises with the higher primates (simians): Is it possible that the New World monkeys (platyrrhines) descended directly from North American prosimians, independently of the origin of Old World monkeys (catarrhines)? If that were the case, the eventual similarity between the two groups of higher primates would have been due to convergent evolution. But this hypothesis was rapidly abandoned because of the closeness of the resemblance. Yet South America, the exclusive zone of diversification of New World monkeys, separated from Africa more than 100 million years ago. So it must be accepted that, with direct migration ruled out, faunal exchange would have required animals rafting from island to island on mats of vegetation. The fossil form found in Bolivia could have originated from Africa in this way.

Living primates are divided into three groups:

- Strepsirrhines (lemurs and lorises), which have an extensive geographical distribution in Madagascar, Africa, and Asia. In comparison with other primates, they exhibit primitive characters, such as a less developed brain (usually with the cerebellum exposed dorsally), a more elongated snout, a temporal fossa, or opening, confluent with the orbit (giving the skull a characteristic impression of having "eyeglasses"), more lateral orbits, the presence of inguinal teats (located low on the belly) in some, three-cusped upper molars in many cases, procumbent lower incisors (forming a scoop at the front of the mandible), and the presence of a claw on the second toe. But in comparison with other mammals they show certain "evolved" characters, such as a somewhat enlarged brain, flat nails on almost all digits, and a tendency toward a vertical body posture.

- Tarsiers, which occur in Southeast Asia. Species in this intermediate group have forward-facing orbits with almost complete separation from the temporal fossa by a bony partition and disappearance of the impression of "eyeglasses." Because of their intermediate status, tarsiers have been classified in two different ways. In traditional classifications, retention of certain primitive features led to the inclusion of tarsiers with lemurs and lorises in the suborder Prosimii; therefore these primates are often collectively called "prosimians." In subsequent classifications designed to reflect evolutionary relationships more directly, tarsiers have been combined with higher primates (monkeys, apes, and humans) in the suborder Haplorhini because of shared ancestry; this is the approach adopted in the formal classification used in the next section of this book.

- Higher primates (simians), which have spread to occupy intertropical regions, even those with quite low temperatures, around the globe except in Madagascar, Australia, and New Zealand. The members of this more highly evolved group are characterized by greater development of the brain, shortening of the snout in most cases, complete isolation of the orbit from the temporal fossa (giving the forward-facing eye sockets a rounded, cuplike form), and generally flat nails on all digits.

This introduction focuses particularly on lemurs because this assemblage of primates provides a simple and almost complete model of the evolution of a discrete zoological group.

Evolution of Madagascar's Lemurs

In spite of the fragility of the hypotheses proposed to explain the origin of lemurs, this group of primates offers a unique opportunity for analysis and investigation. And we must

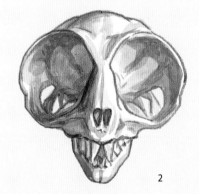

Comparison of the eye sockets (orbits) in the three main groups of living primates:

1. open orbits reminiscent of eyeglasses in lemurs and lorises (sportive lemur)
2. orbits almost enclosed in tarsiers (Spectral Tarsier)
3. orbits completely enclosed in simians or "higher primates" (talapoin)

profit from this now, as it will soon be too late because of the rapidity of destruction of natural habitats by human populations.

Following the breakup of the supercontinent of Gondwana, Madagascar was eventually separated from Africa by a channel some 250 miles wide. Exposed fragments of dry land probably remained for some time between the two landmasses. It can be imagined that the ancestors of the Malagasy lemurs arrived by sea, borne on rafts of vegetation, and that they subsequently diversified in isolation on Madagascar. In the absence of favorable winds and currents, such colonization was probably an extremely rare event.

Malagasy prosimians, or lemurs, represent an *adaptive radiation* that probably took place within the confines of the island. This term describes an assemblage of forms, presumably derived from a common origin that developed through successive modifications of individual characters. In reality, no character evolves in isolation. There is a network of inseparable characters, and we cannot state whether one serves to lead the others. Reconstructions reveal evolutionary trajectories with an assembly of characters progressively accentuated along them—for example development of the brain or specialization of the limbs for leaping. According to competing interpretations, these trajectories are developed either intrinsically, as a property of the group under consideration, or as an apparent result of selection pressure. It is easy to imagine that a given type of animal may establish itself in an environment with abundant resources, where it faces no obstacles, then multiply and diversify in an exuberant manner, effectively radiating from its initial origin.

Nowadays, Madagascar is the only country where such a diversity of prosimians, by far the richest in the world, has been miraculously conserved. There are no fossils dating from the Eocene on this island. But the diversity of lemurs alive today, together with those represented as subfossils (fossilized very recently), is such that their origin must presumably date back at least that far. It seems likely that in a few places on Madagascar habitats similar to those in which primates initially evolved still exist. Such habitats contain numerous forms that can still be observed living in their particular contexts.

Investigation of the physiology of lemurs as well as behavioral observations complement the study of fossils in seeking an understanding of the mechanisms underlying the diversification of the species concerned. Interpretation necessarily plays a major part, but we must try to keep as close as possible to the facts derived from precise observations in order to make those interpretations as plausible as possible.

A Brief History of Evolution

The radiation with very ancient roots that took place on the great island of Madagascar probably began in a relatively limited zone. Many lemur genera coexist in a very confined area, matching in extent the primate radiations in Africa, Asia, and South America, which took place in regions that are vastly greater in size.

Original adaptations are found in many domains. In anatomical terms, the lemurs exhibit a great variety of forms:

- small-bodied mammals with an elongated body form (dwarf lemurs), running along large branches like small carnivores scurrying over flat terrain;
- small-bodied runners-and-leapers that move around rapidly but tire quickly, such that they must find shelter without delay (lesser mouse lemurs);
- specialized leapers with legs distinctly longer than their arms (fork-crowned lemurs, Coquerel's Mouse Lemur);
- leapers that no longer engage in running, with broad, strong thighs (sportive lemurs) or with long, slender thighs (woolly lemurs);

Diversity in body form of lemurs according to their mode of locomotion:
1. Greater Dwarf Lemur (*Cheirogaleus major*)
2. Gray Mouse Lemur (*Microcebus murinus*)
3. Coquerel's Mouse Lemur (*Mirza coquereli*)
4. Eastern Woolly Lemur (*Avahi laniger*)
5. Ring-tailed Lemur (*Lemur catta*)
6. Verreaux's Sifaka (*Propithecus verreauxi*)

- quadrupedal leapers (true lemurs, bamboo lemurs);
- large-bodied leapers with long legs, a vertical trunk, and a very mobile head (sifakas, Indri).

Subfossils—preserved remains of species that died out only recently, so the bones remain unmineralized—are often larger than forms still alive today. (This is hardly surprising, as the skeletons of small animals are much more fragile and hence less likely to be preserved.) Subfossil species found on Madagascar are related to bamboo lemurs, true lemurs, or Indris, and in some the skull has a more "simian" appearance.

Variation among lemurs also exists at the physiological level: Some species are able to accumulate substantial fat reserves and to enter torpor during the season of shorter day length, either for several months (dwarf lemurs) or intermittently for a few days at a time (lesser mouse lemurs). Reproduction is seasonal in all lemurs, with copulation occurring when day length is short or increasing and birth taking place after a gestation period that varies according to the body size of the species concerned. The offspring may be deposited in a nest and carried in the mother's mouth if need be (lesser mouse lemurs, dwarf lemurs). They may also be left clinging to a branch (bamboo lemurs) or spend the first weeks curled around the mother's belly (Ring-tailed, brown, and variegated lemurs, collectively called the true lemurs, and sifakas).

All lemurs have well-developed vision, regardless of whether they are diurnal (Indris, sifakas, and true lemurs) or nocturnal (small-bodied species, like mouse lemurs and dwarf lemurs, and medium-sized species such as sportive lemurs and woolly lemurs). Some medium-sized species in fact have an intermediate kind of pattern known as cathemerality, in which activity occurs both during the night and during the day (bamboo lemurs, brown lemurs). Lemurs also show a remarkable degree of variation in vocalizations and in scent-marking glands. The level of diversity found in prosimians greatly exceeds that found among higher primates.

The types of social organization found in Malagasy lemurs are also very diverse. Nocturnal species (dwarf lemurs; mouse lemurs; sportive lemurs) show little gregarious behavior. Their social interactions are limited to recognition of neighbors, which are rarely approached other than to breed or fight. Nonetheless, they can form sleeping groups, particularly during the winter months, when they may gather in tree holes for a period of torpor. Diurnal lemurs live in family groups (Indris, bamboo lemurs) or in larger troops (Ring-tailed Lemurs). Species represented by large-bodied subfossils were presumably comparable, having diurnal habits and living in social groups.

Microcebus murinus

It has been inferred that animals derived from the African fauna reached Madagascar on rafts of vegetation. Here, the Gray Mouse Lemur (*Microcebus murinus*), which still occurs abundantly in Madagascar's forests, is of special interest. Cytogenetic studies of chromosome structure have yielded indications that this tiny, relatively primitive nocturnal lemur, or an allied precursor, could be close to the origin of the adaptive radiation in Madagascar. There, the common ancestor would have been far less exposed to predators, notably raptors, which were probably far more abundant in Africa than in Madagascar at the time.

Highly adaptable animals such as lesser mouse lemurs were quite able to survive in limited land areas. Indeed, they might even have been isolated on land fragments lying between Africa and Madagascar before reaching the coast of their new island home. Despite the small size of the rafts that would have borne them, they would have been able to find food easily by seeking out fruits and larvae living beneath bark and to cling to tiny branches. Hollows in trunks would have provided shelter. Moreover, the physiological capacities of *Microcebus*, like those of its close relatives the dwarf lemurs (*Cheirogaleus medius* and *Cheirogaleus major*), would have provided special resistance to the effects fasting during the winter season. Uniquely among primates, they can become lethargic for long periods. Their internal temperature then responds to variations in ambient temperature, while their energy expenditure is kept very low. They are hence easily able to survive under difficult conditions. Indeed, dwarf lemurs can remain completely lethargic for several months inside a tree trunk or huddled among roots.

Once they became isolated in their hypothetical landing zone in Madagascar, the *Microcebus* precursors doubtless multiplied rapidly. In captivity, if they are well fed, modern *Microcebus* can breed easily, giving birth to two, three, or sometimes even four offspring a year. For such small mammals they have a relatively long life span, and individuals have lived for more than ten years in the Laboratoire d'Écologie at the Muséum National d'Histoire Naturelle near Paris. Furthermore, they seem to be perfectly at home in almost any kind of natural vegetation and can even survive in cultivated areas, such as coffee or clove plantations. *Microcebus murinus*, marked by its great vitality, seems to be hardier than its larger-bodied and more specialized relatives, which are far more vulnerable to habitat destruction.

The Current State of the Radiation

In Madagascar, tropical rain forest is found in the east, dry deciduous forest in the west, and semiarid spiny forest in the south and southwest. More than thirty lemur species belonging to several families containing thirteen or fourteen genera have been recognized:

- one or two families of small-bodied nocturnal species (four or five genera, depending on the classification adopted), weighing eighty to five hundred grams;
- one family of medium-sized nocturnal species (one genus containing at least five species or subspecies), weighing about one kilogram;
- one family of somewhat larger-bodied diurnal species (four genera), weighing between one and four kilograms;
- one family containing one medium-sized nocturnal genus, weighing one to two kilograms, and two large-bodied diurnal genera, weighing four to five kilograms
- one family of medium-sized nocturnal species (just one genus), weighing two to three kilograms.

The radiation also includes the known subfossil forms, which belong to nine genera distributed among the extant families.

Living alongside this primate fauna are insectivores, rodents, and carnivores, which are themselves representatives of an ancient and very diversified array. Some members of these other radiations went extinct one to two thousand years ago. Contemplating the evolution of nature in Madagascar leads us to believe that without the recent arrival of humans bringing destruction in their wake, many species belonging to the subfossil fauna that have been discovered would still be living in the forests and savannas on the island. It has been estimated that about fifteen lemur species disappeared after humans arrived.

Representation of Primates in the Rest of the World

The closest relatives of the Madagascar lemurs include the bushbabies, prosimians living in central and southern Africa. Bushbabies show similarities to Malagasy species of the genus *Microcebus*, but as yet no fossil link between the two groups has been discovered. Systematists distinguish between them on the basis of certain features of the skull.

Lorises, other prosimians related to bushbabies, have a wide geographical distribution in Asia. Their ancient origin is still undocumented, but they are very closely related to the pottos and angwantibos of equatorial Africa. Paleontological studies in Asia will perhaps reveal a link between the African species and their widely distributed counterparts in Madagascar, such as mouse lemurs, dwarf lemurs, and fork-crowned lemurs.

Fossils linked to bushbabies and pottos were recently discovered in the Fayum region of Egypt, while deposits in Pakistan have yielded a few teeth that may belong to a genus closely related to dwarf lemurs.

In Africa and Asia, prosimians were exposed to competition with higher primates and did not gather the adaptive momentum seen in Madagascar. Africa is the richest continent for primates. Four families are very widely distributed: Galagidae (bushbabies), Lorisidae (pottos and angwantibos), Cercopithecidae (cheek-pouched monkeys), and Hominidae (great apes; sometimes placed in family Pongidae). The cheek-pouched monkeys have differentiated to yield numerous species. In Asia, primates are less diverse. Three of the families that are found there have representatives in Africa, bearing witness to the occurrence of migration between the two continents.

The radiation of primates in South America is the youngest, apparently having taken place over the last twenty-five million years or so. Although prosimians are known as fossils from North America, no representatives are found today in South America. Correspondingly, the diversity of forms occurring there is more limited than on the other continents.

The Role of the Forest and Primate Adaptation

The Impact of the Environment

The trajectory of primate evolution, originating from a remote reptile stock, is utterly remarkable. After their predecessors underwent extreme differentiation through adaptation to life in trees, a group that returned to terrestrial life attained the ultimate development of the brain. This evolutionary trajectory was driven by natural selection.

As the French anthropologist André Langaney has pointed out, by the time of Charles Darwin's birth the French anthropologist Jean-Baptiste Lamarck had already published his *Philosophie Zoologique*. Many of the ideas later formulated by Darwin had already been set out more or less clearly by Lamarck. Therefore, these two precursors should remain associated in our memory for their major contribution to the history of the evolution of species. Across the ages, no better explanation than theirs has been provided toward understanding on a global scale the evolution of species, and the "choices" made by "Nature" in the possible diversity of forms and characters.

In the course of their development, the different life forms that resulted through successive genetic variations were constantly exposed to the "sieve of the environment." Individuals that, for one reason or another, cannot adapt to ambient conditions are rapidly eliminated. The sieve may involve a physical feature, such as a harsh climate, or a biological factor, such as the presence of a successful competitor or a dangerous predator. Depending on the selective factor, elimination will take place more or less rapidly. If its action is not too brutal, the species adapts by exploiting available possibilities. In this way, the mouse and dwarf lemurs in Madagascar and the bushbabies in Africa, by conserving a completely nocturnal way of life, have survived the pressure from predators.

The sieve favors species that adopt territorial defense, a form of behavior that simultaneously permits the limitation and the protection of populations, their food, and their reproductive stages. In effect, it ensures protection of environmental resources while avoiding overexploitation.

The Forest Habitat

From the outset, tropical forest—a habitat characterized by almost incessant productivity—favored the success of the primate group. In tropical rain forests, primates can garner fruits, leaves, or insects throughout the year. At certain privileged sites that represent veritable "laboratories of evolution," such as the remaining areas of tropical forest in Madagascar and Africa, it is still possible to observe this rich production of resources and their utilization under conditions close to those experienced by the first primates. One can infer the evolutionary trajectories of the different species through observations of their home ranges, of interspecific competition, and of predation pressures, while at the same time assessing the diversity and abundance of their food sources. The rain-forest habitat thus offers the possibility of diversification to the animals that live there, reducing competition and favoring the emergence of new species.

Primates occupy all zones of the forest: the crowns of giant trees with abundant flowers and insects, large branches laden with various leaves and fruits, more open and sunlit patches invaded by a specific kind of vegetation, damper patches on slopes receiving little sunlight and on the banks of streams, as well as thickets close to the ground and large dead trunks that have crashed down through the mass of vegetation. As every available ecological niche may be occupied, competition is reduced and diversity becomes established. Rain forest is richer in species than dry forest. Flooded forest, for example in Amazonia, and mangrove forest also provide a home for different primate species, but these forest types are distinctly less common.

Diversification takes place in every functional realm: physical and physiological performance, daily and annual activity rhythms. On Madagascar, one can find up to seven or eight primate species within the same forest area, with bodies ranging between the sizes of *Microcebus* and *Indri*. They also live alongside other mammal species that offer little competition, such as insectivores, rodents, and bats. In some Asian forests, up to eight primate species can be found living in the same area; in Africa, up to seventeen may occur! At any given site, the level of diversity shown by other mammals parallels that of primates.

The abundance of primate species is maximal in equatorial regions and decreases with increasing latitude, paralleling the abundance of plant species. If comparisons are

Worldwide, one of the greatest diversities of higher primate species coexisting in the same habitat is found in the Ituri forest of the Democratic Republic of Congo. Primates from different levels in the forest, shown, from left to right and top to bottom: *Piliocolobus foai oustaleti, Colobus angolensis cottoni, Colobus guereza occidentalis, Cercopithecus ascanius schmidti, Cercopithecus denti, Cercopithecus mitis stuhlmanni, Lophocebus albigena johnstoni, Perodicticus potto, Galago senegalensis, Cercocebus agilis, Cercopithecus neglectus, Cercopithecus lhoesti, Cercopithecus hamlyni, Pan troglodytes schweinfurthi, Papio anubis.* (Adapted from *Histoire naturelle des primates d'Afrique centrale,* by Annie Gautier-Hion, Marc Colyn and Jean-Pierre Gautier, Ecofac, 1999.)

made between different continents at the same latitudes, the same kinds of plant habitats are found: rain forest, dry forest that loses at least part of its leaf cover in winter, thin bands of gallery forest lining the banks of rivers, wooded savannas, and semiarid or arid zones. As a rule, the types of animals that live in these different habitats are analogous, and faunal diversity is broadly comparable. However, the primates inhabiting the forests of South America show less diversity than their counterparts in Africa and Asia. The Neotropical primate fauna includes few exclusive folivores (leaf-eaters), no really large-bodied species, and only one nocturnal genus. In comparison with Africa, there is little cohabitation of closely related species. This phenomenon is perhaps linked to the fact that the evolutionary radiation of New World monkeys, dating back only twenty-five million years or so, is far less ancient than the radiations of primates on other continents.

Adaptation to the Environment

Members of the evolutionary radiation of primates, which that has taken place exclusively in forests, necessarily exhibit adaptations for arboreal locomotion. Such locomotion must be rapid, requiring adaptation of the hands and feet for grasping branches and a compatible body weight. In simians, the forelimb is often better developed than the hind limb. There is a tendency toward arm-swinging—a locomotor specialization of primates that permits them to move around suspended beneath branches. This tendency is fully expressed in some New World monkeys (howler monkeys, spider monkeys, woolly monkeys). By contrast, in prosimians, apart from *Daubentonia* (Aye-aye) and certain subfossil lemurs such as *Palaeopropithecus*, the hind limb is commonly better developed. A tendency toward leaping is evident (Coquerel's Mouse Lemur, fork-crowned lemurs, and sportive lemurs with an elongated ankle region; indrids with an elongated femur). But there is no hind limb dominance in lorisiforms and *Daubentonia*. Among primates generally, the form of the hand and foot is very variable. The digits may bear claws (Aye-aye; marmosets and tamarins), the feet may be long, with a short tarsus (ankle region), the fingers may bear flat nails, and the thumb may become progressively emphasized while the index finger is greatly reduced (lorisids).

In regions that are permanently humid, such as eastern Madagascar or equatorial Africa, trees grow to considerable heights and provide an extensive network of horizontal branches, veritable thoroughfares for moving animals. In regions that are dry for part of the year, trees are not as tall and tend to become bare periodically. In very dry regions, the vegetation becomes spiny, losing the classic types of leaves and bearing small, scale-like leaves, and adopts the form of candelabras, lacking horizontal branches. The lemurs of

Madagascar have become very well adapted to this type of vegetation (Didiereacae). In this kind of forest, sifakas, in particular, move around by leaping from one trunk to another, presenting a magnificent spectacle as their white fur flits across the blue sky.

Increase in Body Size

As evolution progresses, increasing body size of species often occurs. This trend is favored by accompanying energy savings: Heat loss is diminished, because the surface area of the body does not increase in proportion to its volume. Accordingly, animals living in cold climates tend to be bigger than their counterparts in hot countries (Bergman's Law). The American puma provides a perfect illustration. Individuals living in northern Canada and in southern Argentina are bigger than those occupying the central zone of this mammal's range of distribution. Most primates live in tropical regions, but it is precisely among large-bodied species that certain representatives (chimpanzees, gorillas, gibbons, baboons, macaques) have occupied regions that are cold in winter, for example mountainous areas.

When forest-living animals increase in body size, adoption of a vertical body posture facilitates leaping from trunk to trunk, as can be seen in the indri family. While certain small-bodied representatives have also already evolved toward a vertical body posture, it is only in large-bodied species that the efficiency of moving around by leaping can really be appreciated.

The tendency to adopt a vertical body posture is accompanied by a series of anatomical modifications:

- location of the foramen magnum beneath the skull;
- increase in volume of the skull, which is finely balanced on the trunk and well placed for expansion of the brain;
- development of the rib cage;
- shortening of the snout and forward orientation of the eyes.

Increased body size and the type of locomotion that accompanies it permit the animals concerned to escape from predators that are incapable of moving around in this way.

As body weight increases, locomotion demands ever-increasing muscular force. Leaps of fifteen to thirty feet, the limit attained by *Indri* in Madagascar, are not without danger in the forest types that these primates inhabit. When pursued, Indris flee by leaping from trunk to trunk, until fatigue compels them to descend to the ground without much change in mode of progression. They then exhibit a hopping pattern of locomotion intermediate between arborealism and bipedalism, which is generally performed by leaping primates with long legs.

Acquisition of a good leaping technique requires a long, hazardous learning period. As a result, young animals frequently face accidents as they begin to become independent. If a youngster falls, it cannot escape from a quadrupedal predator on open ground. This point is revealingly illustrated by a Malagasy legend, which describes *Indri* parents throwing their offspring to see whether they are able to survive by grabbing at branches. It is quite possible that the leaping mode of locomotion may lead to miscarriages if a pregnant female faces repeated disturbances toward the end of pregnancy. The panic induced by low-flying helicopters passing over the forest, which are increasingly common in Madagascar, may be an important factor in the decline seen in certain subspecies of *Propithecus* (sifakas).

The increase in weight accompanying greater body size has repercussions for an animal's lifestyle and diet, ruling out use of the branch tips, where fruits produced by a tree are generally located. Such animals are left with fruits that grow directly on the trunk, such as those of the breadfruit tree, which are readily eaten. Sifakas living in the forests of southern Madagascar can spend hours on the ground collecting fallen fruits, such as those of tamarind trees, which are a favored food. While on the ground, they leap around bipedally, with the body held vertically and the arms raised above the head. This bounding technique allows them to proceed rapidly to reach the safety of trees in the forest. Ring-tailed Lemurs also spend considerable amounts of time on the ground.

New World monkeys are predominantly arboreal and, with only a few exceptions such as capuchin monkeys, do not usually descend to the ground. By contrast, several species of Old World monkeys, such as baboons and Patas Monkeys, have become very well adapted for terrestrial life and climb up into trees only to rest.

Arm swinging is not found at all among the extant lemurs of Madagascar. In primates that do use this locomotor pattern, the forelimbs, particularly the lower arms, are markedly elongated. This limb adaptation is the opposite of that seen in leapers. The champions among arm-swingers are the gibbons and the Siamang, which exhibit true brachiation. Orangutans and spider monkeys use a less athletic form of this kind of locomotion. Arm-swinging favors an erect body posture, but this evolutionary trajectory has a great drawback in that it monopolizes use of the hand.

In a forest habitat, arboreal animals can move around only on substrates that are relatively firm, but the current level of exploitation and degradation of forests is so extreme that large trees are disappearing. The forests of Madagascar were once far richer than they are now, as is evident from the publications of French naturalists Alfred Grandidier and Charles Lamberton. This explains the earlier existence of Malagasy lemur species, documented by subfossil remains, that were markedly heavier than those alive today. The skull sizes of various subfossil lemurs (*Archaeolemur, Hadropithecus, Mesopropithe-*

cus, *Palaeopropithecus*, *Daubentonia robusta*) ranged between 10 percent larger and twice the size of their modern relatives. Indeed, skulls of the different species of the extinct lemur genus *Megaladapis*, which are reminiscent of the skulls of hoofed mammals, are ten times greater in volume than those of the largest-bodied modern lemurs. The form of their limbs indicates that they were in fact arboreal species. They could certainly move across the ground as well, as is the case with *Indri*, *Propithecus*, and *Daubentonia* on Madagascar today, and as is true of baboons and apes in Africa and Asia. Independently of human activity, a reduction in the presence of large trees in forests could have led to the first locomotor specializations in ancestral indrids, leading them to leap from trunk to trunk instead of moving around on branches. Large-bodied lemurs did have a predator to face, as a viverrid of the genus *Cryptoprocta* that was much bigger than the modern Fossa (*Cryptoprocta ferox*), existed on Madagascar at the time.

For Asian and African species that live mainly on the ground, trees still represent shelter. Indeed, gray langurs in India almost never leave the crowns of trees, where they gorge on leaves until they resemble females close to giving birth. Chimpanzees also use the crowns of trees, building their nests there.

Only gorillas feel at ease on the forest floor, as their size is sufficient to intimidate predators. Terrestrial life is less dangerous for animals like them that have an impressive size. Nevertheless, particularly at night, even they might be surprised by a predator. Consequently, many primate species that are adapted for terrestrial life seek out trees or even rocks on which to sleep, as is the case with Hamadryas Baboons in Ethiopia. Every evening these baboons proceed slowly across a rocky area with steep cliff faces. They move as a group, led by dominant males. These males, veritable leaders, settle down where they can, even leaving some of the best places for others. Some individuals, clinging to a rocky outcrop, do not sleep very well, but no terrestrial predator can reach them.

Certain other species also live in extreme habitats where predators are rare, for example Patas Monkeys or Gelada Baboons, which, like Hamadryas Baboons, are very jealous and keep their females continually close by, using force if necessary.

Hamadryas Baboons (*Papio hamadryas*) spend the night high up on steep rock faces to protect themselves against predators.

Predators

It is in the immediate interest of any individual to avoid predators, but the latter nevertheless play a positive role in maintaining equilibrium in the environment.

Among others, two economists—Thomas Malthus followed by Alfred Sauvy—demonstrated that any population that develops without limits will destroy its habitat and thus production of the food it needs to survive. For example, we know that after overgrazing the productivity of the soil may take several years to regenerate. Hence, the notion of the limitation of population growth becomes vitally important. Seen in this light, predators are indispensable to the survival of the overall system. Moreover, as far as individual species are concerned, predators exert an inevitable pressure on their evolution, ruling out differentiation in directions that are too diverse. In describing the behavior of a species in its habitat, it is therefore essential to seek the predator.

In most cases, a predator lives at the expense of several species, focusing on smaller prey to make it easier to obtain food. Nonetheless, evolution may drive a predator to specialize in a hunting pattern that is adapted for a particular species. Yet such a predator then finds itself in a difficult situation because it depends on a single species. A case in point is the Monkey-eating Eagle (*Stephanoaetus coronatus*) of Africa, which can swoop down suddenly to snatch any imprudent monkey in its talons but is completely committed to this elusive food source.

Madagascar is inhabited by a very efficient predator of lemurs, the Fossa (*Cryptoprocta ferox*). If we pass over its primitive characters, it looks like a small panther that can run and leap very rapidly, both on the ground and among the branches.

Small, agile mongooses, such as *Galidia* and *Galidictis*, run along branches and attack mouse and dwarf lemurs, among other prey. But lemurs may be able to escape them by leaping into vegetation or seeking refuge in hollow tree trunks, making capture difficult.

Raptors are formidable predators for small-bodied lemur species. Despite their agility, lesser mouse lemurs, which are similar in size to the rodents generally preyed upon by the Barn Owl (*Tyto alba*), may fall victim to the owl's very efficient hunting technique. Thanks to its exceptional system of localization using sonar, the owl can detect the lemurs precisely and swoop down noiselessly in the middle of the night. Judging from the abundance of skull fragments found in its regurgitated pellets, this predator, which surely arrived quite recently in Madagascar, is responsible for the demise of many lesser mouse lemurs. In forests that have not suffered too much degradation, these losses are compensated for by the high reproductive output of these lemurs, but it has to be asked whether the evolution of these small-bodied species would have been able to take place if this alien intruder, a very specialized owl, had appeared much earlier in Madagascar.

The main predators of the Malagasy lemurs:

1. Fossa

2. Ring-tailed Mongoose

3. Narrow-striped Mongoose

4. Barn Owl

Defensive and Repellent Strategies

The forest habitat, which is so variable in its composition—with the presence of trees of varying heights, lianas, bark, dead wood, humus, all kinds of leaves—favors rapid flight and concealment. Small-bodies species can take refuge on fine branches that are inaccessible to large carnivores. African talapoin monkeys, which are excellent swimmers, will even drop into water if danger threatens.

Among the small-bodied prosimians of Africa, certain slow-moving species have developed original defensive techniques. Take, for example, the potto (*Perodicticus*), a nocturnal prosimian that is typically solitary and moves slowly around on branches foraging for insects, small reptiles, and fruits. It can grasp firmly, thanks to adhesive pads on its digits, while the nape of its neck bears a shield formed from well-developed cervical spines covered with thick skin. If attacked by a carnivore, it will assail its adversary with a series of bites and parries with the shield that may induce it to flee.

In Asian forests, the slender loris (*Loris*) also moves around slowly and is capable of strong grasping. This prosimian possesses repellent glands beneath its arms and, when it senses danger, rears up and utters a loud hissing noise as well. In the dim nighttime light, undulating movements of its body combined with the markings on its head give the impression of a cobra.

As a result of such extreme specialization, although it is needed for immediate survival, these species are doubtless locked into an "evolutionary cul-de-sac." With that degree of differentiation, it is difficult for them to evolve further by modifying such a pronounced series of anatomical specializations.

It is worth mentioning an original strategy found in nocturnal woolly lemurs (*Avahi*), which live in family groups containing three or four individuals and sleep huddled together in the fork of a tree hidden in foliage. At the slightest alarm, the group abruptly disperses, with each individual leaping rapidly from branch to branch in a different direction, completely disorienting the predator (and the observer as well). In any case when arboreal primates are moving along branches in a closely familiar area, they are generally prey whose capture is energetically expensive for mammalian predators. Unlike primates, these predators lack the well-honed locomotor and visual skills acquired by constantly grasping objects precisely or firmly clutching branches for leaping.

Among the Malagasy lemurs, the bamboo lemur (*Hapalemur*) is the one that most resembles medium-sized monkeys. Because of its size, it is exposed to predators, including carnivorous mammals, birds, and snakes. It doubtless manages to avoid predation fairly effectively because of its drably colored pelage, its cathemeral habits, its movement through a dense cover of foliage, and its social organization into family groups in which young individuals remain during their first year of life.

Defensive postures of a Bosman's Potto (*Perodicticus potto*) and of a Common Slender Loris (*Loris tardigradus*), whose facial mask resembles the hood of a cobra.

The discreet coloration of small-bodied primate species provides them with camouflage in the forest. In fact, as predominantly nocturnal prosimians they have no need for displays of color. Large-bodied species are able to do without such obligatory camouflage. They evolved to become diurnal in habits and more variable in coloration. There is actually a link between their color and their degree of exposure to sunlight. The need for protection from the sun results in a pale-colored pelage, whereas a dark color maximizes the benefit from heat absorption if only weak sunlight is available. The Old World monkeys of Africa, whose classification reflects wide variation in color patterns, developed this diversity in response to local climates with very varied incidence of sunlight.

Overabundance of Predators

Excessive predation has catastrophic effects. For instance, three million years ago more dynamic predators belonging to the fauna of North America were able to invade South America when the Isthmus of Panama was formed. Subsequently, in the southern region—which had long remained isolated and had become home to an endemic, well-balanced fauna that was able to exploit its habitat without destroying its productivity—many animal species disappeared.

The survivors were mainly limited to certain species adapted to an arboreal environment, such as members of the primate radiation, as no North American carnivore was able to pursue them efficiently among the branches. Perhaps the development of specialized prehensile (grasping) tails in certain New World monkeys (*Alouatta*, *Ateles*, *Brachyteles*, *Lagothrix*), permitting them to move around securely in the crowns of the highest tress, coincided with the timing of this invasion.

From the perspective of nature conservation, instead of studying such rare natural catastrophes, it would seem to be more interesting and also more urgent to consider stable natural habitats, such as those that were conserved on Madagascar before people arrived and which still exist in a few intact areas. In such a habitat, predators and prey evolved in parallel, thus becoming harmoniously complementary, and there was no brutal shock to trigger extinctions.

A predator belonging to the group of arboreal viverrids, close to the ancestor of today's mammalian carnivores and related to the Fossa, landed on Madagascar at the same time as the first lemurs and also underwent an evolutionary radiation. This relatively unspecialized animal, which was able to survive exclusively on fruits and insects, like lemurs, or to hunt for small vertebrates, was doubtless easily able to cope with transportation on a raft, thanks to its physiological adaptations. Once it became established in its new living quarters, a process of speciation (formation of new species) would have led it to hunt new arboreal prey, such as the small species of nocturnal lemurs. Little by little, several forms of this predator would have evolved.

As a result, we can perhaps observe a predator-prey equilibrium that emerged long ago, with each predator species adapted to particular prey. From the very beginning of their expansion, thanks to trees, primates have been able to benefit from a precious advantage that allowed them to evolve slowly and smoothly in tandem with their predators.

Primate Territories and Social Organization

A social lifestyle is advantageous for resisting predation because the group is quickly alerted if a predator appears on the scene. On the other hand, adoption of a social lifestyle requires an environment that is relatively rich in food supply. For herbivorous animals, this does not pose much of a problem.

The Habitat Zone

For each animal species studied in a given environment, ethologists define a "home range" representing the zone regularly visited by an individual, family, or larger social group. This constitutes the space required for feeding and rearing offspring. A "family" of lesser mouse lemurs (the mother and her young of the year), for example, depends on plant and animal resources yielded over a year by approximately two and a half acres of forest, although the actual size varies from one forest to another.

Most primates are essentially vegetarian, although some small-bodied species (tarsiers, Demidoff's Bushbaby) provide exceptions to the rule. The home range required to provide food for individual primate species varies between about 25 and 250 acres. Species that actively forage for animal prey have larger home ranges.

The "territory" is a zone that resident individuals energetically defend against intruders of the same species. Here, too, the area concerned varies from species to species. In fact, mouse and dwarf lemurs of Madagascar, African bushbabies, Asian lorises and other quasi-solitary prosimians live in territories that may overlap. A male may visit the territories of several females and block access to rivals.

Diurnal primates predominantly live in social groups, in which case the territory is shared by group members. The social structure of the group regulates population density according to the richness of the habitat. The organization of any given social system must ensure long-term persistence. So integration into social groups simultaneously provides defense against predators and protection of the natural habitat.

Among the Malagasy lemurs, small-bodied species are nocturnal and generally occupy individual territories, whereas larger-bodied species are diurnal and live in families or larger groups. Increase in body size is hence accompanied by a transition from a dispersed type of social organization to a gregarious type, which is more compatible with conservation of the habitat.

Social Organization

Patterns of social organization are extremely variable among primates. Species may live:

- solitarily, with males and females ranging separately over territories that overlap to a considerable degree (bushbabies, pottos, lesser mouse lemurs, orangutans);
- in pairs, with a male and female coordinating their activities in the same territory, regardless of breeding season (Indris, titi monkeys, gibbons);
- in permanent associations of more than two adult males and a number of females. Individuals move around together, but the structure of the group is quite variable (brown lemurs, howler monkeys, spider monkeys, guenons, macaques, chimpanzees).

According to the species and the area inhabited, such larger groups generally include between half a dozen and fifty individuals. Changes in group composition occur relatively frequently, particularly when young adults emigrate. The existence of groups in which more females than males are present can result in formation of bachelor groups composed solely of males. Males and females are born in equal number, so a certain number of males are in any case excluded and live on the fringe of the zone inhabited. Peripheral males are mistreated to varying extents and badly nourished, easily falling prey to predators. However, from time to time a peripheral male may replace an established male in a group.

There are no solitary species among New World monkeys. In Africa, by contrast, only solitary and group-living species seem to occur. In Madagascar, nocturnal lemur species live solitarily or in pairs; they never form larger groups.

Some primate genera include both pair-living and group-living species (*Hapalemur*, *Eulemur*, *Varecia*, *Cebuella*, *Leontopithecus*, *Saguinus*, *Nasalis*, *Presbytis*). *Tarsius* is the only genus that contains solitary and pair-living species.

The manner in which mothers take care of their offspring is closely connected to the type of social group in which they live. Any female that moves around with a large group has to carry her offspring with her from birth onward, and the infant is adapted to cling to her fur. With solitary primates, by contrast, the offspring can remain in a nest while the mother is absent.

With both New World and Old World monkeys, one can encounter larger groups containing individuals of different species, which visit the same abundant fruit sources together. Although they may not communicate intentionally, each species understands the signals (especially vocalizations) uttered by the others, and this bestows benefits for predator avoidance.

Primate Sociability and Recognition Signals

Large-bodied species that live in social groups have greater cerebral capacities and a higher degree of socialization. Later attainment of maturity by their offspring permits a more extended learning period. The sophisticated development of social primates is associated with greater individual value of every member of a group.

Vocal communication, notably when involved with maintenance of the territory, is extremely important.

Vocal Communication

Primates have very well developed hearing combined with efficient communication. Indeed, their survival often depends on perceiving sounds and interpreting the significance of alarm calls. Immediate flight is a response triggered by alarm calls, which seemingly incorporate quite detailed information such as the source of danger, the direction in which to flee, and so on.

If danger threatens, small-bodied species with no special form of defense generally limit their vocal signals or, as in the case of *Microcebus murinus*, communicate with ultrasound, the source of which is more difficult for unspecialized predators to localize.

High-frequency vocalizations are rapidly attenuated in forest vegetation. However, they are perfectly suited to the small territories of lesser mouse lemurs, which can circumvent the masking effect of natural sounds by varying the frequency of the calls emitted. The animals are notably alert when hearing is hampered by wind and rain. However, in an extended territory, as is found with large-bodied species that have less to fear from predators, low-frequency calls are more effective because of their better penetration in the forest.

Vocal communication plays a key part in group cohesion. It is an amusing sight to observe a group of diurnal lemurs in a state of alarm. Dispersed among the branches, all looking in the direction from which danger has been detected, they swing their tails to-and-fro while uttering aggressive, anxious grunts that will rise to a crescendo if the threat continues. African guenons do the same thing.

This behavior is well understood by other species living in the same area. These kinds of displays, which are likely to intimidate a predator, are of no value to certain medium-sized species such as *Hapalemur occidentalis* in Madagascar or *Miopithecus talapoin* in Africa. In their case, an alarm call or discreet vocalizations suffice to signal danger and to trigger flight.

The observer of primates notices that the same calls regularly occur under particular circumstances. It is hence possible to classify vocalizations into categories by observing the behavior of individuals at the time of emission. Any repetitive pattern may be considered to serve some useful purpose for a species, if not for the individual itself. Sound recording with a tape recorder followed by frequency analysis of calls reveals relatively limited vocal repertoires that differ little between closely related species.

The calls of very young animals are adapted to the behavior of adults. In many cases, the squeal of a lemur separated from its mother is powerful and affects the whole social group, which responds to the alarm by preparing to ward off a predator. By contrast, a young bamboo lemur—an animal that habitually remains immobile and inconspicuous on a branch—signals its presence with a discreet call when its mother approaches.

The most frequently used vocalizations are those uttered in the context of alarms; these may be emitted when one individual rejects contact with another, to signal territory ownership, or in response to distress. With discreet species, such as bamboo lemurs, there is a category of faint, repetitive calls that signal presence in the group to other individuals without alerting other species or predators in the locality. This kind of vocal emission, which varies in frequency and intensity rather like a language, provides information on activity of group members. If the group is relatively dispersed, calling is louder. Alarm calls also resemble language in communicating the seriousness of the threat and even, it seems, its nature, distinguishing the approach of a terrestrial predator from that of an aerial attacker. If the danger increases, the entire group calls in unison.

As the size of territories increases, territorial vocalizations become louder. With a minimum of effort, they signal to neighbors that the area is occupied, inhibiting any intent to move in. In fact, it is interesting to note that intimidation calls emitted by an entire group are very similar in vocal structure to territorial calls. They hence serve two functions: defense against predators, for example by scaring away overzealous raptors that sometimes seek to capture offspring close to their mothers, and maintenance of territories by contributing to spatial organization and population limitation.

In certain primates, powerful calls are amplified by the presence of special vocal organs:

1. howler monkey
2. Indri
3. Siamang

These two functions became increasingly important as evolution progressed, with certain consequences. For example, the security of a group increases as the number of individuals capable of signaling danger grows. This evidently promotes social life and, in its wake, patterns of communication become more diversified.

In the same way, rejection of contact is expressed by vocalizations that are initially faint but gradually increase in strength. Territorial calls are one manifestation of this. On the other hand, the distress call, which signals the presence of mortal danger, is rarely used. A specific kind of call is also observed during sexual activity.

All the types of vocalizations, which number about fifteen, exhibit many variants and intermediate forms. Increasing experience with these variants reveals their significance, which is actually quite limited.

The main example of a vocal repertoire discussed here was studied in the bamboo lemur (*Hapalemur*). Such repertoires have also been recognized in many Old World and New World monkeys. Territorial calls are the most varied. In some genera (*Indri*, *Alouatta*, *Hylobates*, *Pongo*), special vocal organs facilitate the production of the calls, greatly increasing their power. The territory concerned is generally very large. A fifteen-year-old male orangutan can make himself heard at a distance of one to two miles and provoke any young males in the vicinity to flee.

"The great lemurs of the earliest time on Earth, perhaps our most distant ancestors . . . began to sing their invisible and melancholy calls, with strange sounds of another world, resembling those of denizens of the sea, made audible by amplification." This passage from the novel *Les Flamboyants* by Patrick Grainville is evocative of the call of Malagasy Indris (sometimes called "dogs of the forest"). Their calls are produced by the entire group and can be heard over half a mile away in any direction. It is also reminiscent of the sportive lemurs' doleful call—it can hardly be called a song—which signals their presence by night at some considerable distance through the forest. In western Madagascar, fork-crowned lemurs and Coquerel's Mouse Lemurs similarly celebrate nightfall with salvos of powerful vocalizations.

Just by observing the behavior of the lesser mouse lemur, which possesses a large "vocabulary" of relatively simple ultrasonic calls, one can already sense the importance that language would attain over the course of primate evolution. The conquest and mastery of articulated sounds with a lower frequency represents the beginning of the development of a "language" capable of transmitting the elements of "culture."

But there is a long, long road from practical mastery of emissions of sound and ultrasound to use of language! Quite generally, the following conclusion can be drawn from an understanding of the evolution of mammals: Even if communication with sounds becomes progressively more complex, it always boils down to a relationship with perception at the instant in which the sounds are experienced.

Recognition by Odor

Olfactory signals are numerous and varied in primates. They may serve to help an individual recognize a locality, analyze an object, or assess the ripeness of a fruit. But, particularly in prosimians, they can also correspond to the marking of a site or, more rarely, of a partner, which is done using a secretion with a characteristic and persistent odor.

Small-bodied nocturnal species such as mouse and dwarf lemurs of Madagascar and African bushbabies—the least evolved primates—use olfaction extensively. It serves in the recognition of territorial marking by deposition of urine and feces or secretions of specialized glands.

Many mammals, particularly carnivores, perform scent-marking with urine or feces. It is the most rudimentary form of marking and is also found in all primates. Both *Microcebus murinus* and *Galagoides demidoff* will urinate in one hand and then rub it on a branch (urine washing). A true lemur will rub the top of its head, impregnated with urine, on a branch or on the fur of one of its companions. With *Cheirogaleus*, which avidly consumes very ripe fruits, it is the feces that are dragged along a branch with the base of the tail. The anus is located right at the root of the tail, enabling the feces to be spread along the main pathways that an individual follows in its territory.

Marking with the secretion from a specialized gland located close to body orifices (anal, urinary, genital) is also very widespread and may be accompanied by urine marking. In *Microcebus murinus*, the male marks his territory by rubbing his scrotal glands against a support, and *Eulemur fulvus*, *Cheirogaleus*, *Hapalemur*, *Propithecus*, and *Avahi* show the same behavior. *Mirza coquereli* bolsters this kind of marking by emitting puffs of odor from time to time.

Some primate species are characterized by specialized pectoral or brachial glands. Glandular formations coupled with specialized structures (a brush or horny spur) help to anchor an odor more durably. Two glands are clearly visible in *Hapalemur occidentalis*, one on the inner side of the forearm, augmented by a zone of horny papillae forming a kind of brush, and the other on the front of the shoulder. These two glands are brought into contact by flexing the arm at the elbow, allowing the mixed secretions to impregnate the brush. The animal then rubs this structure against a branch and, with a sweeping motion powered by the entire body, produces veritable scars on the bark, through which the secretion penetrates. *Lemur catta* also employs special glands located on the arms, at the base of its neck, or below the chin. While clinging to a tree trunk, a sifaka rubs its neck gland on the bark with extended vertical thrusts of its body, stopping from time to time to sniff the marking site. Several New World monkeys have pectoral marking glands. Marking can also be carried out with saliva, in which case the animal bites the substrate.

The vomeronasal organ (Jacobson's organ), located beneath the scroll-like turbinate bones in the nasal cavity, participates in the detection of odors. Its role seems to be detection of particular chemical substances by virtue of its well-developed sensory cells. However, this organ has almost disappeared in humans. By contrast, we have often observed how a lemur, with its nose pressed against a tree, will spend considerable time "reading" a scent message impregnated there.

In the larger-bodied primate species, the role of olfaction is eclipsed by the visual sense. This is particularly true of the genera *Erythrocebus*, *Macaca*, *Papio*, *Theropithecus*, *Gorilla*, and *Pan*.

In the anthropoid apes (gibbons, orangutans, gorillas, and chimpanzees), marking behavior is more discreet and approaches the condition seen in humans. Olfaction seems to have less importance under normal circumstances. However, a tame young orangutan whose behavior I was able to study under favorable conditions would habitually pull my hand toward his nose every time I went to visit him.

In humans, the olfactory sense has regressed, at least at the conscious level. But some traces of it apparently persist in certain forms of behavior. For example, certain Mediterranean hip-swaying dances are reminiscent of group marking. In one, the man shakes a scarf impregnated with the odor of his armpits near his partner. Many sayings also allude to olfactory sensations, linking them to emotional responses involved in attraction or rejection of contact with an individual, who is either likable or "stinks."

In various human populations, transmission of odor from the armpits is involved in gestures of farewell. However, all of these practices are rapidly disappearing in the wake of modern civilization, which works in the other direction by favoring the suppression of individual odors.

Tactile Communication

Monkeys and apes depend on feeling through touching, not only with the hand, as expected, but also with the muzzle, the tongue, and even the teeth. In anthropoid apes, the well-developed lower lip is used extensively for this purpose.

The term *grooming* is universally employed to refer to a raking movement of the fingers through a neighbor's fur. (The corresponding French word is *toilettage*.) Higher primates (simians) show this behavior far more than the prosimians. The latter perform the same action with the lower incisor teeth, the horizontal crowns of which form a kind of scoop. (In fact, this is the same dental array that allows them to pierce and scrape the pulp of fruits on which they feed.)

In lemurs, the body areas cleaned during grooming bouts are primarily the arms and the head, and the behavior really serves for delousing, as ectoparasites are removed in this way. Monkeys and apes seem to perform this activity only after a thorough visual examination and careful reflection.

In fact, in a group of monkeys or apes grooming takes place continually, and its social function is clearly evident. It occurs whenever there is a threat of conflict to signal attempted reconciliation. In habitual use, it indicates bonds between individuals of either sex and reflects a peaceable relationship. Surely our handshakes, caresses, and social kisses belong in the same category.

Touching is the most direct message of appeasement. It is, in effect, a physical expression of the social bond. It cannot be ignored, whereas a vocal message, although it can be commanding, is less immediate and may more often be addressed to a group of individuals. As far as visual signals are concerned, they seem to be the most discreet and refined of all, and the most difficult to recognize.

Advantages and Disadvantages of a Social Lifestyle

Maintenance of a social group demands persistent signals that serve the indispensable cause of reconciliation. Conciliatory signals are developed to varying degrees in different species, and of course those that have the fewest exhibit the most serious degrees of aggression and injury.

In a monkey or ape society, at any given time the general behavior of individuals depends on the composition of groups of "allies." An individual rarely faces an aggressor alone, because relatives and allies provide support if the conflict escalates. If two individuals are involved in a dispute, a third can play a conciliatory role.

But social life entails supplementary constraints. The hierarchy within the group is unlikely to be universally acceptable. So we are led to inquire, following Dutch ethologist Jan Van Hooff, what benefit an individual derives from social life. The most obvious advantage is more effective defense against predators, thanks to the numerous signals and alarms that are elicited by a group. Thus it is that protection of young individuals increases with the size of the social group. This compensates for the fact that female fertility seemingly declines with group size. The question of foraging for food is more ambiguous. Food sources are indeed more easily detected, but the individual is then exposed to competition within the group.

As a final point, primate societies have traits that we can recognize because they characterize human societies everywhere: the inescapable existence of a "boss" and a corresponding struggle to occupy that position; the feeling of well-being that doubtless ensues from social living; and the need for harmony among group members, which makes reconciliation and appeasement indispensable because, on the other side of the river or simply beyond the forest clearing, there is the "other" group.

Primate Intelligence

People are fascinated by the mental capacities of monkeys and apes. Several attempts have been made to teach artificial languages to apes, especially chimpanzees.

Human language is, in effect, a code employing symbols. Without these, according to the American anthropologist-linguist Edward Sapir, the development and refinement of thought would have been impossible. Some research workers (notably at the Yerkes Center at Emory University in Atlanta, Georgia, devoted to the study of primates) accordingly designed a code of communication using symbols to represent various objects, mainly related to food and drink. Although this approach is fairly remote from use of a real language, certain chimpanzee test subjects exhibited a remarkable memory capacity. It is in any case worth noting that such training requires the subject to display a capacity for attention that is surely absent from small-bodied primate species.

Perhaps we should heed the words of a Malagasy woodcutter: "If they do not speak, it is because they do not have anything special to say!"

In fact, the goal of such research is not to teach a language to a chimpanzee in the hope that he will give us his point of view about the world. The aim is to find out first of all whether he is capable of using symbols and then, using a battery of tests designed for the purpose, to explore his faculties for discriminating notions such as "identical" and "different." Once this has been achieved—that is, when the "word" has been assimilated—the next step is to employ that capability in a variety of contexts. According to David Premack, an American psychologist working on animal intelligence, only primates are capable of this feat. And it should not be forgotten that apes that have become famous in such studies—Sarah, Washoe, Koko, and so on—have never been able to achieve 100 percent success despite their excellence as pupils!

In traditional fashion, tests are based on obtaining a food reward, reflecting a primordial feature of animals generally: The gesture of pressing a button or a pedal to obtain a tasty morsel at a given place is quickly learned, even by lesser mouse lemurs (and many other animals besides).

Various other tests permit evaluation of the mental capacities of primates. For example, after watching objects being hidden, test subjects must then uncover them, or they must respond to a novel object being presented in a familiar place, and so on. During such tests, young animals always show themselves to be more active and rapidly responsive than adults. Some chimpanzees have shown the capacity to recognize themselves in a mirror.

Among the capacities that primates have shown during testing, the most surprising is that of concealing their intentions by diverting the attention of the trainer, or persuading a conspecific to move away in order to remain alone with a reward. This level of mental sophistication is almost incredible!

To classify primates, we first need to identify and list the various populations that inhabit different habitats around the globe, and then we must group them according to their similarities and evolutionary relationships. (The classification presented in this book is restricted to nonhuman primates.) A biological classification is initially based on the observation of physical characters. Each animal described receives a **genus** name and a **species** name. The latter distinguishes it from any adjacent population that is recognizably different. If there are only minor distinctions in morphology or color, a **subspecies** is created. This is often the case in forest habitats where one geographical region is separated from another by a natural barrier such as a river.

The genus (plural *genera*) groups together populations that share many physical characters. These may not always be externally visible; for example they may involve skeletal anatomy or the dentition.

Genera are then grouped into **families** and families sometimes into **superfamilies**. Additional subdivisions, such as **subfamily** or **subgenus**, allow further refinement of groupings.

A classification hence expresses degrees of relationship and depends on the choices that are made regarding the characters on which it is based and the value attributed to them.

Following more detailed study, a genus may be "revised," and the populations it contains are then redistributed. This sometimes leads to creation of new genus names for particular populations. By contrast, the species name is more stable. It may be complemented with a subspecies name, which may in due course be transformed into a species name; but this name usually persists and preserves a link to the existence of the population concerned.

Recently, the study of characters that are not immediately visible, such as the chemical structure of components in the cell nucleus, has permitted the discovery of previously hidden relationships among populations, thus leading to additional revisions.

If a species has a wide distribution, we can expect to find numerous geographical forms that may become separate species. A listing of such species for they genera in which they are prevalent (*Cercopithecus*, *Macaca*, *Callithrix*, *Saguinus*, and so on) reflects the dazzling diversity of these groups of primates.

The different groups of primates are not uniformly distributed across the continents. Some groups have flourished in certain regions, whereas others have been unable to establish themselves there. Thus it is that Madagascar is occupied by the great majority of prosimians to the exclusion of other primates, that South America is home to all the platyrrhines in the world, to the exclusion of other higher primates, and that Australia is completely lacking in nonhuman primates while Africa and Asia (as well as Europe and North America in the past) harbor representatives of both prosimians and catarrhines. These distributions are connected with geography and the possibilities for passage from one region to another.

The **abbreviated classification of primate species** presented on pages 40 to 46 is limited to the species illustrated in the plates of this book.

The **dimensions** indicated in the legends to the plates indicate the following measurements: L: body length, from the tip of the snout to the root of the tail. T: length of the tail. W: approximate body weight.

The **maps** show the approximate distribution for each species. Each number refers to the corresponding caption and to the animal's image on a plate. Numbers for subspecies included in the distribution of the principal species are not shown on the maps.

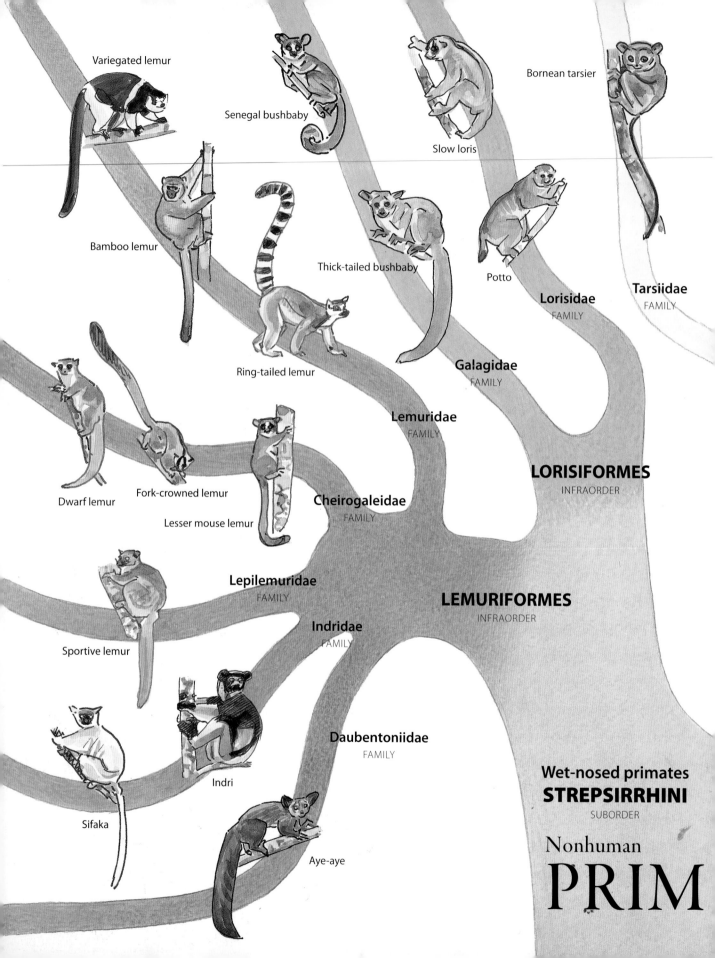

Variegated lemur

Senegal bushbaby

Slow loris

Bornean tarsier

Bamboo lemur

Thick-tailed bushbaby

Potto

Tarsiidae
FAMILY

Ring-tailed lemur

Lorisidae
FAMILY

Galagidae
FAMILY

Lemuridae
FAMILY

LORISIFORMES
INFRAORDER

Dwarf lemur

Fork-crowned lemur

Lesser mouse lemur

Cheirogaleidae
FAMILY

Lepilemuridae
FAMILY

LEMURIFORMES
INFRAORDER

Sportive lemur

Indridae
FAMILY

Daubentoniidae
FAMILY

Indri

Wet-nosed primates
STREPSIRRHINI
SUBORDER

Sifaka

Aye-aye

Nonhuman
PRIM

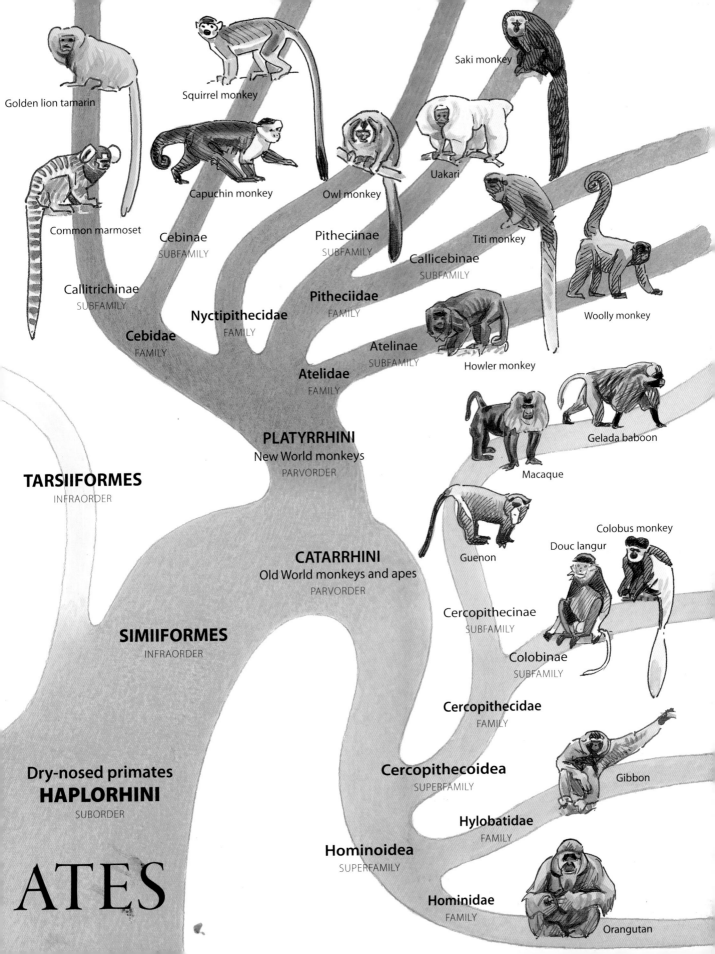

Golden lion tamarin

Squirrel monkey

Saki monkey

Common marmoset

Capuchin monkey

Owl monkey

Uakari

Cebinae
SUBFAMILY

Pitheciinae
SUBFAMILY

Titi monkey

Callicebinae
SUBFAMILY

Callitrichinae
SUBFAMILY

Pitheciidae
FAMILY

Cebidae
FAMILY

Nyctipithecidae
FAMILY

Woolly monkey

Atelinae
SUBFAMILY

Atelidae
FAMILY

Howler monkey

PLATYRRHINI
New World monkeys
PARVORDER

TARSIIFORMES
INFRAORDER

Gelada baboon

Macaque

CATARRHINI
Old World monkeys and apes
PARVORDER

Guenon

Douc langur

Colobus monkey

SIMIIFORMES
INFRAORDER

Cercopithecinae
SUBFAMILY

Colobinae
SUBFAMILY

Cercopithecidae
FAMILY

Cercopithecoidea
SUPERFAMILY

Dry-nosed primates
HAPLORHINI
SUBORDER

Gibbon

Hylobatidae
FAMILY

Hominoidea
SUPERFAMILY

ATES

Hominidae
FAMILY

Orangutan

SUBORDER
STREPSIRRHINI

INFRAORDER
LEMURIFORMES

SUPERFAMILY
LEMUROIDEA

FAMILY
Cheirogaleidae

GENUS   **Hairy-eared dwarf lemur** – *Allocebus*
1 species | Plate 1 | pp. 48–49
Hairy-eared Dwarf Lemur – *Allocebus trichotis*

GENUS   **Lesser mouse lemurs** – *Microcebus*
17 species | Plate 1 | pp. 48–49
Pygmy Mouse Lemur – *Microcebus myoxinus*
Brown Mouse Lemur – *Microcebus rufus*
Gray Mouse Lemur – *Microcebus murinus*

GENUS   **Giant mouse lemurs** – *Mirza*
2 species | Plate 1 | pp. 48–49
Coquerel's Mouse Lemur – *Mirza coquereli*

GENUS   **Dwarf lemurs** – *Cheirogaleus*
7 species | Plate 2 | pp. 50–51
Fat-tailed Dwarf Lemur – *Cheirogaleus medius*
Greater Dwarf Lemur – *Cheirogaleus major*

GENUS   **Fork-crowned lemurs** – *Phaner*
4 species | Plate 2 | pp. 50–51
Masoala Fork-crowned Lemur – *Phaner furcifer*
Amber Mountain Fork-crowned Lemur – *Phaner electromontis*

SUBORDER
STREPSIRRHINI

INFRAORDER
LEMURIFORMES

SUPERFAMILY
LEMUROIDEA

FAMILY
Lepilemuridae

GENUS   **Sportive lemurs** – *Lepilemur*
24 species | Plate 3 | pp. 52–53
Gray-backed Sportive Lemur – *Lepilemur dorsalis*
White-footed Sportive Lemur – *Lepilemur leucopus*
Red-tailed Sportive Lemur – *Lepilemur ruficaudatus*
Small-toothed Sportive Lemur – *Lepilemur microdon*
Milne-Edwards's Sportive Lemur – *Lepilemur edwardsi*
Weasel Sportive Lemur – *Lepilemur mustelinus*
Northern Sportive Lemur – *Lepilemur septentrionalis*

SUBORDER
STREPSIRRHINI

INFRAORDER
LEMURIFORMES

SUPERFAMILY
LEMUROIDEA

FAMILY
Lemuridae

GENUS   **Bamboo lemurs** – *Hapalemur*
5 species | Plate 5 | pp. 56–57
Golden Bamboo Lemur – *Hapalemur aureus*
Alaotra Bamboo Lemur – *Hapalemur alaotrensis*
Western Bamboo Lemur – *Hapalemur occidentalis*

GENUS   **Greater bamboo lemur** – *Prolemur*
1 species | Plate 5 | pp. 56–57
Greater Bamboo Lemur – *Prolemur simus*

GENUS   **Ring-tailed lemur** – *Lemur*
1 species | Plate 6 | pp. 58–59
Ring-tailed Lemur – *Lemur catta*

GENUS   **Brown lemurs** – *Eulemur*
11 species | Plates 6–9 | pp. 58–63
Collared Lemur – *Eulemur collaris*
White-collared Lemur – *Eulemur albocollaris*
White-headed Lemur – *Eulemur albifrons*
Red-fronted Lemur – *Eulemur rufus*
Red-bellied Lemur – *Eulemur rubriventer*
Blue-eyed Lemur – *Eulemur flavifrons*
Common Brown Lemur – *Eulemur fulvus*
Mayotte Lemur – *Eulemur fulvus mayottensis*
Crowned Lemur – *Eulemur coronatus*
Sanford's Lemur – *Eulemur sanfordi*
Mongoose Lemur – *Eulemur mongoz*
Black Lemur – *Eulemur macaco*

GENUS   **Ruffed lemurs** – *Varecia*
2 species | Plate 10 | pp. 64–65
Hybrid Black-and-white × Red Ruffed Lemur –
   Varecia variegata × rubra
Northern Black-and-white Ruffed Lemur –
   Varecia variegata subcincta
Variegated Black-and-white Ruffed Lemur –
   Varecia variegata variegata
Southern Black-and-white Ruffed Lemur –
   Varecia variegata editorum
Red Ruffed Lemur – *Varecia rubra*

SUBORDER
STREPSIRRHINI
INFRAORDER
LEMURIFORMES
SUPERFAMILY
LEMUROIDEA
FAMILY
Daubentoniidae

GENUS Aye-aye – *Daubentonia*
1 species | Plate 4 | pp. 54–55
Aye-aye – *Daubentonia madagascariensis*

SUBORDER
STREPSIRRHINI
INFRAORDER
LEMURIFORMES
SUPERFAMILY
LEMUROIDEA
FAMILY
Indridae

GENUS Indri – *Indri*
1 species | Plate 11 | pp. 66–67
Northern Indri – *Indri indri indri*
Southern Indri – *Indri indri variegatus*

GENUS Woolly lemurs – *Avahi*
8 species | Plate 11 | pp. 66–67
Eastern Woolly Lemur – *Avahi laniger*
Western Woolly Lemur – *Avahi occidentalis*

GENUS Sifakas – *Propithecus*
9 species | Plates 12 and 13 | pp. 68–71
Diademed Sifaka – *Propithecus diadema*
Crowned Sifaka – *Propithecus coronatus*
Coquerel's Sifaka – *Propithecus coquereli*
Decken's Sifaka – *Propithecus deckeni*
Milne-Edwards's Sifaka – *Propithecus edwardsi*
Perrier's Sifaka – *Propithecus perrieri*
Tattersall's Sifaka – *Propithecus tattersalli*
Verreaux's Sifaka – *Propithecus verreauxi*
Silky Sifaka – *Propithecus candidus*

SUBORDER
STREPSIRRHINI
INFRAORDER
LORISIFORMES
SUPERFAMILY
LORISOIDEA
FAMILY
Lorisidae

GENUS Slow lorises – *Nycticebus*
3 species | Plate 33 | pp. 106–107
Common Slow Loris – *Nycticebus coucang*
Bengal Slow Loris – *Nycticebus bengalensis*
Pygmy Slow Loris – *Nycticebus pygmaeus*

GENUS Slender lorises – *Loris*
2 species | Plate 33 | pp. 106–107
Common Slender Loris – *Loris tardigradus*
Lydekker's Slender Loris – *Loris lydekkerianus*

GENUS Potto – *Perodicticus*
1 species | Plate 51 | pp. 142–143
Bosman's Potto – *Perodicticus potto*

GENUS Angwantibos – *Arctocebus*
2 species | Plate 51 | pp. 142–143
Calabar Angwantibo – *Arctocebus calabarensis*
Golden Angwantibo – *Arctocebus aureus*

SUBORDER
STREPSIRRHINI
INFRAORDER
LORISIFORMES
SUPERFAMILY
LORISOIDEA
FAMILY
Galagidae

GENUS Needle-clawed bushbabies – *Euoticus*
2 species | Plate 52 | pp. 144–145
Southern Needle-clawed Bushbaby – *Euoticus elegantulus*

GENUS Thick-tailed bushbabies – *Otolemur*
3 species | Plate 52 | pp. 144–145
Brown Thick-tailed Bushbaby – *Otolemur crassicaudatus*

GENUS Lesser bushbabies – *Galago*
20 species | Plate 52 | pp. 144–145
Allen's Bushbaby – *Galago alleni*
Demidoff's Bushbaby – *Galago demidoff*
Mohol Bushbaby – *Galago moholi*

GENUS **Crested mangabeys** – *Lophocebus*

3 species | Plate 63 | pp. 162–163

Gray-cheeked Mangabey – *Lophocebus albigena albigena*
Osman Hill's Gray-cheeked Mangabey – *Lophocebus albigena osmani*
Johnston's Gray-cheeked Mangabey – *Lophocebus albigena johnstoni*
Black Crested Mangabey – *Lophocebus aterrimus*

GENUS **Baboons** – *Papio*

5 species | Plates 65 and 66 | pp. 166–169

Olive Baboon – *Papio anubis*
Chacma Baboon – *Papio ursinus*
Guinea Baboon – *Papio papio*
Yellow Baboon – *Papio cynocephalus*
Hamadryas Baboon – *Papio hamadryas*

GENUS **Gelada baboon** – *Theropithecus*

1 species | Plate 66 | pp. 168–169

Gelada Baboon – *Theropithecus gelada*

GENUS **Forest baboons** – *Mandrillus*

2 species | Plate 67 | pp. 170–171

Drill – *Mandrillus leucophaeus*
Mandrill – *Mandrillus sphinx*

SUBFAMILY

Colobinae

GENUS **Southern odd-nosed monkeys** – *Nasalis*

2 species | Plate 38 | pp. 116–117

Pig-tailed Langur – *Nasalis concolor*
Proboscis Monkey – *Nasalis larvatus*

GENUS **Douc langurs** – *Pygathrix*

3 species | Plate 39 | pp. 118–119

Gray-shanked Douc Langur – *Pygathrix cinerea*
Black-shanked Douc Langur – *Pygathrix nigripes*
Red-shanked Douc Langur – *Pygathrix nemaeus*

GENUS **Snub-nosed monkeys** – *Rhinopithecus*

4 species | Plate 40 | pp. 120–121

Black Snub-nosed Monkey – *Rhinopithecus bieti*
Golden Snub-nosed Monkey – *Rhinopithecus roxellana*
Tonkin Snub-nosed Monkey – *Rhinopithecus avunculus*
Gray Snub-nosed Monkey – *Rhinopithecus brelichi*

GENUS **Gray langurs** – *Semnopithecus*

7 species | Plate 41 | pp. 122–123

Tufted Gray Langur – *Semnopithecus priam*
Southern Plains Gray Langur – *Semnopithecus dussumieri*
Nepal Gray Langur – *Semnopithecus schistaceus*
Northern Plains Gray Langur – *Semnopithecus entellus*

GENUS **Lutungs** – *Trachypithecus*

17 species | Plates 42–44 | pp. 124–129

Capped Langur – *Trachypithecus pileatus*
Silvered Leaf Monkey – *Trachypithecus cristatus*
Purple-faced Langur – *Trachypithecus vetulus*
Dusky Leaf Monkey – *Trachypithecus obscurus*
White-headed Langur – *Trachypithecus poliocephalus leucocephalus*
Gray-headed Langur – *Trachypithecus poliocephalus poliocephalus*
Delacour's Langur – *Trachypithecus delacouri*
François's Langur – *Trachypithecus francoisi*
Hatinh Langur – *Trachypithecus hatinhensis*
Javan Lutung – *Trachypithecus auratus*
Phayre's Leaf Monkey – *Trachypithecus phayrei*
Nilgiri Langur – *Trachypithecus johnii*
Gee's Golden Langur – *Trachypithecus geei*

GENUS **Surilis** – *Presbytis*

11 species | Plate 45 | pp. 130–131

Javan Gray Langur – *Presbytis comata*
Yellow-handed Mitered Langur – *Presbytis melalophos melalophos*
Thomas's Langur – *Presbytis thomasi*
Natuna Island Langur – *Presbytis natunae*
Southern Mitered Langur – *Presbytis melalophos mitrata*
Ferruginous Mitered Langur – *Presbytis melalophos nobilis*
Maroon Langur – *Presbytis rubicunda*
Tricolored Langur – *Presbytis femoralis cruciger*

GENUS **Black-and-white colobus monkeys** – *Colobus*

5 species | Plate 68 | pp. 172–173

Tanzanian Black-and-white Colobus Monkey – *Colobus angolensis palliatus*
Ursine Colobus Monkey – *Colobus vellerosus*
Kilimanjaro Guereza – *Colobus guereza caudatus*
Congo Guereza – *Colobus guereza occidentalis*
Mount Kenya Colobus Monkey – *Colobus guereza kikuyuensis*
Black Colobus Monkey – *Colobus satanas*
King Colobus Monkey – *Colobus polykomos*

GENUS **Red colobus monkeys** – *Piliocolobus*

9 species | Plate 69 | pp. 174–175

Upper Guinea Red Colobus Monkey – *Piliocolobus badius badius*
Central African Red Colobus Monkey – *Piliocolobus foai oustaleti*
Pennant's Red Colobus Monkey – *Piliocolobus pennantii*
Temminck's Western Red Colobus Monkey – *Piliocolobus badius temminckii*
Zanzibar Red Colobus Monkey – *Piliocolobus kirkii*

GENUS **Olive colobus monkey** – *Procolobus*

1 species | Plate 69 | pp. 174–175

Van Beneden's Olive Colobus Monkey – *Procolobus verus*

Primates by Continent

PLATES AND DESCRIPTIONS OF SPECIES

LEMURIFORMES

LEMUROIDEA

Cheirogaleidae

Mouse and dwarf lemurs, which include five genera, have dense, woolly fur, three pairs of teats, and notably large eyes. The eyes, which are typical for nocturnal strepsirrhine species, possess a layer of cells, constituting the *tapetum lucidum*, that reflect light and enhance vision at night. These primates, which are all arboreal, move around in trees by running and leaping. The home range, which varies from five to twelve and a half acres according to species and region inhabited, is generally shared by one male and several females. Although their vocalizations are primarily composed of high-frequency sounds, they are quite varied. During the mating season in September–October, the males' testes increase in volume four- or five-fold. In winter, during the Madagascar dry season, several dwarf lemur species hibernate. Their metabolism slows, and they stop eating and enter a kind of torpor that lasts between five and six months.

Mouse Lemurs

GENUS *Allocebus* | **Hairy-eared dwarf lemur** | 1 species | Plate 1

Hairy-eared Dwarf Lemurs live in a very localized, small zone of the northeastern rain forest close to Antongil Bay. They feed on insects, fruits, and sap and other exudates of trees and lianas. They hibernate in tree hollows in which they build nests with leaves. They are much more rare than lesser mouse lemurs and are severely threatened by deforestation. They were reported to be extinct, but in the 1990s a small population was rediscovered. The skull of this species is entirely different from that of a mouse or dwarf lemur, but in some respects resembles that of a fork-crowned lemur.

GENUS *Microcebus* | **Lesser mouse lemurs** | 17 species | Plate 1

Lesser mouse lemurs include the smallest living primates. *Microcebus myoxinus* holds the featherweight record, averaging about an ounce (thirty grams), which explains how it earned its name of Pygmy Mouse Lemur. With the advent of the cold season, lesser mouse lemurs start to lay down fat reserves, especially in the tail region, by increasing food intake. In this way, they can double their weight before reducing activity during the off-season. In contrast to the Dwarf lemurs, however, they do not hibernate. Lesser mouse lemurs lead relatively solitary lives, although the home ranges of different individuals overlap extensively. They mark their territories abundantly with urine and scented secretions from special glands. This kind of marking serves not only to deter rivals but also, in females, to signal sexual receptivity to surrounding males at the appropriate time.

GENUS *Mirza* | **Giant mouse lemurs** | 2 species | Plate 1

Giant mouse lemurs, which are distinctly larger than lesser mouse lemurs, live in dry forests, where they feed on fruits, flowers, sap, and insects and other small invertebrates. At certain times their diet is predominantly composed of sugary exudates from small sap-sucking insects related to aphids and mealybugs. Coquerel's Mouse Lemurs reduce their activity during the cold season, but they do not accumulate any fat reserves to survive this period.

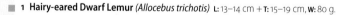

1 **Hairy-eared Dwarf Lemur** (*Allocebus trichotis*) **L:** 13–14 cm + **T:** 15–19 cm, **W:** 80 g.

2 **Coquerel's Mouse Lemur** (*Mirza coquereli*) **L:** 20 cm + **T:** 33 cm, **W:** 305 g.

3 **Brown Mouse Lemur** (*Microcebus rufus*) **L:** 12.5 cm + **T:** 11.5 cm, **W:** 50 g.

4 **Pygmy Mouse Lemur** (*Microcebus myoxinus*) **L:** 6 cm + **T:** 10 cm, **W:** 30 g.

5 **Gray Mouse Lemur** (*Microcebus murinus*) **L:** 12.5 cm + **T:** 13.5 cm, **W:** 109 g.

LEMURIFORMES

LEMUROIDEA

Cheirogaleidae

Dwarf and Fork-crowned Lemurs

GENUS *Cheirogaleus* | **Dwarf lemurs** | 7 species | Plate 2

Dwarf lemurs scurry through the forest at night seeking the fruits and insects on which they feed. They run along branches, frequently marking them with streaks of feces and urine. They accumulate abundant fat deposits before hibernating between April and September to November (according to species), reawakening at the onset of the rainy season. They are the only primates that enter true hibernation. During this period of lethargy, their body temperature falls by about forty degrees to only 60°F, and they lose about half of their body weight. They are solitary and meet up only during the mating season. After a gestation lasting about two and a half months, the female gives birth to two or three offspring that she will carry around in her mouth for the first three weeks, until they are able to move independently and follow her around. To communicate with one another, dwarf lemurs utter defensive snorts and whistling calls.

GENUS *Phaner* | **Fork-crowned lemurs** | 4 species | Plate 2

Fork-crowned lemurs are distinguished from other members of the family Cheirogaleidae in having longer hind limbs than forelimbs. This is connected with the fact that these primates are particularly well adapted for leaping. This is their preferred means of locomotion in the primary and secondary forests where they live. They are solitary or live in pairs, occupying a home range extending over about ten acres. Males have glands located on the neck, which serve to mark females with their odor rather than to establish the boundaries of their territories. These lemurs feed on fruits, flowers, and secretions of insects related to aphids and mealybugs, along with large quantities of sap and other exudates from trees and lianas. During the daytime, they sleep in hollow tree trunks or in leaf nests. Fork-crowned lemurs emit several kinds of powerful vocalizations, with the male and female calling in a duet.

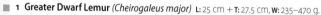

1 **Greater Dwarf Lemur** *(Cheirogaleus major)* L: 25 cm + T: 27.5 cm, W: 235–470 g.

2 **Fat-tailed Dwarf Lemur** *(Cheirogaleus medius)* L: 20 cm + T: 20 cm, W: 140–215 g.

3 **Masoala Fork-crowned Lemur** *(Phaner furcifer)* L: 23–28 cm + T: 28–37 cm, W: 460 g.

4 **Amber Mountain Fork-crowned Lemur** *(Phaner electromontis)* L: 23–28 cm + T: 28–37 cm, W: 460 g.

LEMURIFORMES

LEMUROIDEA

Lepilemuridae

Sportive lemurs, which total twenty-four different species all belonging to the single genus *Lepilemur*, are distributed throughout almost all forests in Madagascar. They are closely related to *Megaladapis*, large-bodied terrestrial subfossil lemurs weighing between 90 and 180 pounds that lived on the island three thousand years ago. Sportive lemurs are nocturnal, strictly territorial primates that are exclusively herbivorous and feed only on leaves, fruits, seeds, barks, and flowers.

Sportive Lemurs

GENUS *Lepilemur* | **Sportive lemurs** | 24 species | Plate 3

Sportive lemurs are nocturnal. They move around either slowly by climbing on branches or rapidly with a series of leaps from trunk to trunk. They achieve this by extending their powerful hind limbs while maintaining the body in a vertical position. They feed primarily on leaves and flowers and reingest their feces in the same way rabbits do. They have small home ranges that are effectively territories and defend them by signaling their presence with numerous varied advertisement calls and by fighting with neighbors. In certain areas where they are not hunted by local people, their population densities can reach 75 to 150 individuals per square mile.

Sportive lemurs mate between May and August. Gestation lasts five months. The single infant, born between October and January, is unable to cling to the mother's fur and is deposited in a nest, in a tree hollow, or on a branch until it can move around and accompany its mother.

1 **White-footed Sportive Lemur** *(Lepilemur leucopus)* L: 25 cm + T: 25–27 cm, W: 540–580 g.

2 **Milne-Edwards's Sportive Lemur** *(Lepilemur edwardsi)* L: 28 cm + T: 28 cm, W: 1 kg.

3 **Small-toothed Sportive Lemur** *(Lepilemur microdon)* L: 35 cm + T: 30 cm, W: 1 kg.

4 **Weasel Sportive Lemur** *(Lepilemur mustelinus)* L: 35 cm + T: 30 cm, W: 1 kg.

5 **Red-tailed Sportive Lemur** *(Lepilemur ruficaudatus)* L: 28 cm + T: 21 cm, W: 800 g.

6 **Northern Sportive Lemur** *(Lepilemur septentrionalis)* L: 28 cm + T: 25 cm, W: 700 g.

7 **Gray-backed Sportive Lemur** *(Lepilemur dorsalis)* L: 25 cm + T: 27 cm, W: less than 1 kg.

8 *Lepilemur* subspecies not illustrated.

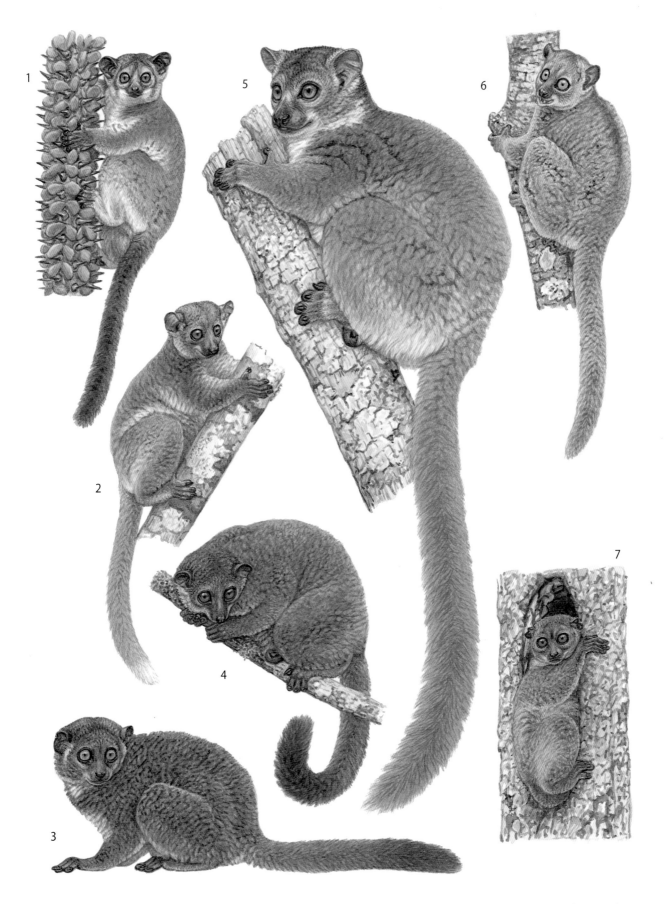

LEMURIFORMES

LEMUROIDEA

Daubentoniidae

Aye-aye

GENUS *Daubentonia* | **Aye-aye** | 1 species | Plate 4

The aye-aye genus was once represented by a larger-bodied form as well. The existing species has an almost uniformly black pelage. It is clearly distinguished from other lemurs by some very unusual characters, including powerful incisor teeth (just two, rather than four, in upper and lower dentition) and an extremely thin, probe-like middle finger, which is used to dislodge food morsels from small fissures and cavities. The Aye-aye is essentially nocturnal and moves around by walking along branches and sometimes across the ground. It spends the day sheltered from possible predators in a large nest constructed with twigs. The long, bushy tail has a double function: It provides balance during locomotion and also wraps around the body inside the nest.

The Aye-aye's diet is quite varied, primarily depending on insects, but also including sap and fruits. The animal is very adept at gnawing the shells of coconuts in order to drink the juice before scraping away the pulp with its specialized middle finger. That finger is also used to extract insect larvae from beneath bark, where the Aye-aye can localize them thanks to its big ears and highly sensitive hearing. When surprised, an Aye-aye will emit characteristic two-phased snorts, which are frequently repeated for some while. This species is nocturnal and solitary. Following a gestation of five months, the female gives birth to a single infant, which spends the first weeks after birth sheltered in a nest and remains dependent on its mother for two years.

■ **1 Aye-aye** *(Daubentonia madagascariensis)* **L:** 40 cm + **T:** 40 cm, **W:** 2.5 kg.

1

LEMURIFORMES

LEMUROIDEA

Lemuridae

Although they are mainly diurnal, lemurs in the Lemuridae family are also active for part of the night. They are medium-sized and slender-bodied, and their hind limbs, which are generally longer than the forelimbs, are adapted for leaping. A long tail serves to maintain balance. In many species the infant is able to cling to the mother's fur from birth onward and is carried around by her. Most lemurids live in groups containing several adult males along with several females.

Bamboo Lemurs

GENUS *Hapalemur* | **Bamboo lemurs** | 5 species | Plate 5

Bamboo lemurs are medium-sized and have a red-tinted greenish-brown pelage. One of their main characteristics is connected with their diet, which principally consists of bamboos, accounting for their common name. Although they primarily feed on bamboo shoots, they also feed on stems and mature leaves, which in some species contain high cyanide levels. It is still a mystery how bamboo lemurs neutralize these toxins. In fact, this source of food is notably energy-poor, so they have to ingest a daily ration representing almost a third of their body weight. Bamboo lemurs live in small family groups that occupy territories in dense forest extending twenty-five to two hundred acres. Territorial boundaries are marked with glands located on the lower side of the forearms. After a gestation period lasting about four and a half months, the female gives birth to one or two infants. Infants are carried in the mother's mouth initially, until they are able to cling to her fur, first on her belly and then on her back. Bamboo lemurs emit a large number of vocalizations, ranging from faint, regularly repeated grunts that maintain cohesion of the small family group to powerful and prolonged *creeee* alarm calls.

GENUS *Prolemur* | **Greater bamboo lemur** | 1 species | Plate 5

Greater Bamboo Lemurs are in many respects similar to other bamboo lemurs, but they differ in being essentially nocturnal. Members of this species feed almost exclusively on bamboos in the heart of dense primary forests. They occupy extensive home ranges that may cover up to 250 acres in area. They actively mark their ranges with brachial glands and, in the case of males, with another gland located close to the neck. In order to deposit his odor on branches, the male flexes his forearm toward his shoulder, thus allowing a small brush on the wrist to become impregnated with scent substances secreted by the gland near the neck. He then rubs his arm against a support to mark it. Greater Bamboo Lemurs are more social than other bamboo lemurs. Groups encountered may contain between four and around thirty individuals.

■ **1 Greater Bamboo Lemur** *(Prolemur simus)* **L:** 45 cm + **T:** 44 cm, **W:** 2.1–2.4 kg.

■ **2 Western Bamboo Lemur** *(Hapalemur occidentalis)* **L:** 28 cm + **T:** 30–40 cm, **W:** 1 kg.

▨ **2b** *Hapalemur* subspecies not illustrated.

■ **3 Alaotra Bamboo Lemur** *(Hapalemur alaotrensis)* **L:** 28 cm + **T:** 30–40 cm, **W:** 890–930 g.

■ **4 Golden Bamboo Lemur** *(Hapalemur aureus)* **L:** 40 cm + **T:** 40 cm, **W:** 1.5 kg.

LEMURIFORMES

LEMUROIDEA

Lemuridae

Ring-tailed and Brown Lemurs

GENUS *Lemur* | **Ring-tailed lemur** | 1 species | Plate 6

The genus *Lemur* contains only one species, the Ring-tailed Lemur, which is probably the best known of all the lemurs. These diurnal primates live in large troops including between twenty and thirty individuals led by a dominant female. Their territories, occupying fifteen to fifty acres or more, are fiercely defended against rival groups. They are bounded by multiple scent marks that are applied to tree trunks and branches with glands located on the underside of the lemur's forearms and around the genital organs. Moreover, dominant females unhesitatingly launch violent attacks on their neighbors, and it is not uncommon for infants to fall or be mortally wounded during such fights. Odors are also very important during the mating season. Males engage in veritable "stink fights," frenetically waving above rivals' heads their long, ringed tails impregnated with odors from the forearm. Ring-tailed Lemurs are very vocal and use a large repertoire of calls ranging from a powerful alarm call to a faint mewing vocalization that helps to maintain group cohesion.

GENUS *Eulemur* | **Brown lemurs** | 11 species | Plates 6–9

The genus *Eulemur* includes eleven species that are all quite common and widely distributed across Madagascar. They are all mainly diurnal, but may also be active part of the night. In most species, the pelage is sexually dichromatic, being distinctly different between males and females, especially with respect to color. An extreme form is seen in the black lemur: The male alone has an ebony-colored pelage, while the female's fur is predominantly brown, with white on the belly and around the ears. All species are group living, although group sizes range from a few individuals to about twenty, according to species. Boundaries of home ranges are marked with scent glands. Brown lemurs eat a wide array of foods, including fruits, flowers, leaves, seeds, bark, and sap, in addition to various insects and small vertebrates. One notable food source is provided by poisonous millipedes, which Red-bellied Lemurs eat after rubbing them between their hands to remove their toxic secretions.

■ **1 Red-bellied Lemur** (*Eulemur rubriventer*) **L:** 40 cm + **T:** 50 cm, **W:** 2.1–2.3 kg.

■ **2 Ring-tailed Lemur** (*Lemur catta*) **L:** 42 cm + **T:** 60 cm, **W:** 2.7 kg.

1 ♂

1 ♀

2

2

LEMURIFORMES

LEMUROIDEA

Lemuridae

Brown Lemurs

GENUS *Eulemur* | **Brown lemurs** | 11 species | Plates 6–9

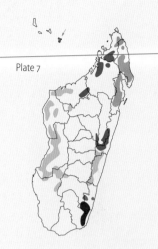

Plate 7

Plate 7

■ **1 White-headed Lemur** *(Eulemur albifrons)* **L:** 39–42 cm + **T:** 50–54 cm, **W:** 2–2.6 kg.

■ **2 Sanford's Lemur** *(Eulemur sanfordi)* **L:** 38–40 cm + **T:** 50–55 cm, **W:** 1.8–2 kg.

■ **3 Common Brown Lemur** *(Eulemur fulvus)* **L:** 40–50 cm + **T:** 50–55 cm, **W:** 2.2–2.5 kg.

■ **4 Collared Lemur** *(Eulemur collaris)* **L:** 39–40 cm + **T:** 50–55 cm, **W:** 2.1–2.5 kg.

■ **5 Mayotte Lemur** *(Eulemur fulvus mayottensis)* **L:** 40–50 cm + **T:** 50–55 cm, **W:** 2.1–2.5 kg.

■ **6 White-collared Lemur** *(Eulemur albocollaris)* **L:** 39–40 cm + **T:** 50–55 cm, **W:** 2–2.5 kg.

■ **7 Red-fronted Lemur** *(Eulemur rufus)* **L:** 35–48 cm + **T:** 45–55 cm, **W:** 2.2–2.3 kg.

Plate 8

■ **1 Mongoose Lemur** *(Eulemur mongoz)* **L:** 35 cm + **T:** 48 cm, **W:** 1.6 kg.

■ **2 Crowned Lemur** *(Eulemur coronatus)* **L:** 34 cm + **T:** 45 cm, **W:** 1.7 kg.

Plate 9

■ **1 Black Lemur** *(Eulemur macaco)* **L:** 41 cm + **T:** 55 cm, **W:** 2.4 kg.

■ **2 Blue-eyed Lemur** *(Eulemur flavifrons)* **L:** 41 cm + **T:** 55 cm, **W:** 2.4 kg.

Plate 8

Plate 9

1♀

1♂

2♂

2♀

3♀

3♂

4♀

4♂

5♀

5♂

6♀

6♂

7♂

7♀ +j

1♀ +j

1♂

2♀

2♂

LEMURIFORMES

LEMUROIDEA

Lemuridae

Ruffed Lemurs

GENUS *Varecia* | **Ruffed lemurs** | 2 species | Plate 10

Ruffed lemurs are large-bodied and have a bushy pelage that is strikingly colored with patches of black and white and in some cases brown as well. They are extremely vulnerable to habitat degradation and survive in refuge areas in intact primary forests, where they live in small groups of five to ten individuals. Each group actively defends a territory of about twenty-five acres by means of calls, aggressive intimidatory behavior directed at any intruder, and scent marking of the boundaries. Ruffed lemurs are easily recognized by their alarm calls, powerful barks that carry over long distances. In contrast to most other lemur species, the female ruffed lemur gives birth every year to two infants after a relatively short gestation lasting about one hundred days. For the first few weeks, she leaves the infants protected in a nest made of leaves and hair, until they are able to accompany her by clinging to her fur as she moves around the forest. Ruffed lemurs feed on fruits, seeds, leaves, and nectar. They often suspend themselves head down in trees, like bats, adopting this position most often while feeding.

- ■ **1** **Northern Black-and-white Ruffed Lemur** *(Varecia variegata subcincta)* **L:** 50 cm + **T:** 60 cm, **W:** 3.5 kg.
- ■ **2** **Variegated Black-and-white Ruffed Lemur** *(Varecia variegata variegata)* **L:** 50 cm + **T:** 60 cm, **W:** 3.5 kg.
- ■ **3** **Southern Black-and-white Ruffed Lemur** *(Varecia variegata editorum)* **L:** 50 cm + **T:** 60 cm, **W:** 3.5 kg.
- **4** **Hybrid Black-and-white × Red Ruffed Lemur** *(Varecia variegata × rubra)* **L:** 50 cm + **T:** 60 cm, **W:** 3.5 kg. Not indicated on the map.
- ■ **5** **Red Ruffed Lemur** *(Varecia rubra)* **L:** 50 cm + **T:** 60 cm, **W:** 3.5 kg.

LEMURIFORMES

LEMUROIDEA

Indridae

The indri family contains eighteen species belonging to three genera. All are folivorous, feeding principally on leaves. These lemurs, which occur in almost all of Madagascar's forests, move around by leaping between branches and from trunk to trunk while keeping the body vertical. Most species are diurnal, but woolly lemurs (*Avahi*) differ in being nocturnal.

Indri and Avahis

GENUS *Indri* | **Indri** | 1 species | Plate 11

The Indri, named *babakoto* ("man of the forest") in Malagasy, is the largest of the extant strepsirrhine primates (an assemblage that groups lemurs with bushbabies, lorises, and pottos) and produces songs that are among the most remarkable in the animal kingdom. Its territorial calls resemble long, powerful howls that are both plaintive and harmonious. They are emitted in unison by several members of the group and are often echoed by songs of one or more neighboring groups. Indris live in pairs, accompanied by their offspring. The female, who is dominant over the male, gives birth to a single infant after a gestation period lasting about four and a half months. The species inhabits the northeastern rain forest of Madagascar and feeds essentially on leaves, fruits and seeds. In contrast to all other lemurs, Indris have a very short tail.

GENUS *Avahi* | **Woolly lemurs** | 8 species | Plate 11

Woolly lemurs owe their name to the softness of their dense, bushy fur, which resembles wool. They are nocturnal and spend the day rolled up into a ball and clinging to a branch. They live in pairs, often accompanied by one or two young individuals of different ages. Beneath the chin, they possess glands that produce scent substances used to mark a territory of about five acres shared by the pair. Their call, a kind of modulated, very high-pitched whistle, also serves as a territorial signal.

- **1 Southern Indri** (*Indri indri variegatus*) **L:** 60 cm + **T:** 5 cm, **W:** 7.1 kg (female); 5.8 kg (male).
- **2 Northern Indri** (*Indri indri indri*) **L:** 60 cm + **T:** 5 cm, **W:** 7.1 kg (female); 5.8 kg (male).
- **3 Eastern Woolly Lemur** (*Avahi laniger*) **L:** 29 cm + **T:** 26–27 cm, **W:** 1.3 kg (female); 1 kg (male).
- **4 Western Woolly Lemur** (*Avahi occidentalis*) **L:** 29 cm + **T:** 26–27 cm, **W:** 1.3 kg (female); 1 kg (male).

LEMURIFORMES

LEMUROIDEA

Indridae

Sifakas

GENUS *Propithecus* **Sifakas** | 9 species | Plates 12 and 13

Sifakas, the Malagasy name by which *Propithecus* species are commonly known, are legendary for their grace and elegance, notably when moving bipedally across the ground, like ballerinas performing *pas chassés*. At the beginning of the day, the members of a group expose their bellies to the sun for some while before setting out to forage for food. Their diet consists mainly of leaves, fruits, and bark. They mark their territories with scent glands located beneath the chin, and they also perform marking with urine. Confrontations are frequent at boundaries between neighboring groups and are accompanied by guttural calls resembling barks. The female is sexually receptive only for a few hours. After a gestation lasting about four months, she gives birth to a single infant that she carries clinging to her fur, first on her belly and later on her back.

■ **1** **Crowned Sifaka** *(Propithecus coronatus)* L: 42–50 cm + T: 50–60 cm, W: about 4 kg.

■ **2** **Decken's Sifaka** *(Propithecus deckeni)* L: 42–50 cm + T: 50–60 cm, W: about 4 kg.

■ **3** **Coquerel's Sifaka** *(Propithecus coquereli)* L: 42–50 cm + T: 50–60 cm, W: about 4 kg.

■ **4** **Verreaux's Sifaka** *(Propithecus verreauxi)* L: 42–45 cm + T: 56–60 cm, W: 3.5–3.6 kg.

■ **5** **Tattersall's Sifaka** *(Propithecus tattersalli)* L: 45–50 cm + T: 45 cm, W: 3.3 kg.

LEMURIFORMES

LEMUROIDEA

Indridae

Sifakas

GENUS *Propithecus* | **Sifakas** | 9 species | Plates 12 and 13

■ **1 Milne-Edwards's Sifaka** *(Propithecus edwardsi)* L: 47 cm + T: 50–60 cm, W: 5.9–6.3 kg.

■ **2 Perrier's Sifaka** *(Propithecus perrieri)* L: 42–50 cm + T: 50–60 cm, W: 4–4.4 kg.

■ **3 Diademed Sifaka** *(Propithecus diadema)* L: 48–52 cm + T: 46.5 cm, W: 5.6–7.2 kg.

■ **4 Silky Sifaka** *(Propithecus candidus)* L: 42–50 cm + T: 50–60 cm, W: 4–5 kg.

SIMIIFORMES

PLATYRRHINI

Cebidae

Until recently, most New World monkey species were allocated to this family. But current classifications retain only two subfamilies in the Cebidae.

Callitrichinae

The callitrichines, marmosets and tamarins, constitute the most primitive subfamily of New World monkeys. Apart from the big toe, which is opposable and has a nail, their digits are claw bearing. Despite their archaic appearance, these claws in fact evolved secondarily from nails as a recently developed character. (Nails represent one of the major features that characterize primates as a group.) Secondary evolution of claws from nails is linked to the way of life of marmosets and tamarins, which use their claws to climb trees by clinging to trunks. They also frequently run quadrupedally along horizontal branches and leap between them. Marmosets and tamarins live in small family groups containing up to ten individuals, but only a single female breeds within each group. She generally gives birth to two infants, which are reared cooperatively with other members of the group and often ride on the male's back.

Marmosets

GENUS *Callibella* | **Dwarf marmoset** | 1 species | Plate 14

First described in 1998, Roosmalen's Dwarf Marmoset is the most social of the callitrichines. Groups of some thirty individuals are sometimes seen, including several adult females that are all able to breed, in contrast to other marmosets. Moreover, the dwarf marmoset does not defend a territory. Each female gives birth to a single infant each year and rears it unaided. Reportedly, there are only one hundred or so individuals of this species surviving in a tiny forest area covering just over one thousand square miles in northern Brazil.

GENUS *Callimico* | **Goeldi's monkey** | 1 species | Plate 14

Goeldi's Monkey is the only callitrichine to possess thirty-six teeth, as compared to thirty-two in all other genera. The fur, which is completely black, forms a kind of bonnet on the head. The female gives birth to a single infant after a gestation of five months. Intensive scent marking is performed in the group territory—some 75 to 150 acres in area—both with urine and also with secretions produced by glands located on the chest. The species is quite vocal, emitting seven different kinds of calls.

GENUS *Cebuella* | **Pygmy marmoset** | 1 species | Plate 14

With a body weight no greater than 130 grams, pygmy marmosets are not only the smallest primates in South America but also the smallest monkeys of any kind. They feed predominantly on gums and saps from some forty tree species and around twenty different lianas. During the dry season, they also consume nectar and insects. Group members use their sharpened lower canines and incisors every day to bore holes into the trunks of trees within a territory that extends over little more than an acre. The holes they bore provoke the flow of sap, thus ensuring that they always have something to eat. Pygmy marmosets live in pairs, accompanied by offspring from previous litters. They are often found together with Black-mantled Tamarins (*Saguinus nigricollis*) in mixed groups.

■ 1 **Roosmalen's Dwarf Marmoset** (*Callibella humilis*) **L:** 16.5 cm + **T:** 22.5 cm, **W:** 150–185 g.

■ 2 **Goeldi's Monkey** (*Callimico goeldii*) **L:** 22 cm + **T:** 25–32 cm, **W:** 400–500 g.

■ 3 **Pygmy Marmoset** (*Cebuella pygmaea*) **L:** 13 cm + **T:** 20 cm, **W:** 120–130 g.

SIMIIFORMES

PLATYRRHINI

Cebidae

Callitrichinae

Marmosets

GENUS *Callithrix* | **Atlantic marmosets** | 6 species | Plate 15

The genus *Callithrix* contains six species that are all similar in size and habits, but distinguishable by pelage coloration. Marmosets in this genus possess well-developed lower incisors that are used to bore holes into tree trunks in order to harvest various exudates, such as saps and gums. Most species have tufts of hair alongside the ears and a ringed tail.

GENUS *Mico* | **Amazonian marmosets** | 14 species | Plates 16 and 17

Amazonian marmosets are closely comparable to their Atlantic counterparts in morphology and behavior. They are distinguished from the genus *Callithrix* essentially by their zone of distribution, confined to the Amazon basin as opposed to the Atlantic forest fringe, the refuge for *Callithrix* species.

Plate 15

■ **1 Common Marmoset** *(Callithrix jacchus)* **L:** 18.5 cm + **T:** 28 cm, **W:** 235–250 g.

■ **2 Geoffroy's Marmoset** *(Callithrix geoffroyi)* **L:** 19.8 cm + **T:** 29 cm, **W:** 190 g (female); 230–350 g (male).

■ **3 Black-tufted Marmoset** *(Callithrix penicillata)* **L:** 20–22 cm + **T:** 28–32 cm, **W:** 180 g (female); 225 g (male).

■ **4 Buffy-tufted Marmoset** *(Callithrix aurita)* **L** and **T:** no data available, **W:** 400–450 g.

■ **5 Buffy-headed Marmoset** *(Callithrix flaviceps)* **L:** 23 cm + **T:** 32 cm, **W:** 406 g.

■ **6 Wied's Marmoset** *(Callithrix kuhlii)* **L** and **T:** no data available, **W:** 350–400 g.

Plate 16

■ **1 Gold-and-white Marmoset** *(Mico chrysoleuca)* **L:** 21.5 cm + **T:** 35 cm, **W:** 310 g (female); 280 g (male).

■ **2 Maués Marmoset** *(Mico mauesi)* **L:** 21 cm + **T:** 33–37 cm, **W:** 350 g.

■ **3 Santarem Marmoset** *(Mico humeralifer)* **L:** 21.5 cm + **T:** 35 cm, **W:** 310 g (female); 280 g (male).

Plate 17

■ **1 Silvery Marmoset** *(Mico argentata)* **L:** 21 cm + **T:** 30–32 cm, **W:** 320 g (female); 357 g (male).

■ **2 White Marmoset** *(Mico leucippe)* **L:** 21 cm + **T:** 30–32 cm, **W:** 320 g (female); 357 g (male).

■ **3 Black-tailed Marmoset** *(Mico melanura)* **L:** 21 cm + **T:** 30–32 cm, **W:** 320 g (female); 357 g (male).

■ **4 Satéré Marmoset** *(Mico saterei)* **L:** 21 cm + **T:** 30–32 cm, **W:** 320 g (female); 357 g (male).

■ **5 Rio Acari Marmoset** *(Mico acariensis)* **L:** 24 cm + **T:** 35 cm, **W:** 420 g.

■ **6 Marca's Marmoset** *(Mico marcai)* **L:** 21 cm + **T:** 30–32 cm, **W:** 320 g (female); 357 g (male).

■ **7 Manicore Marmoset** *(Mico manicorensis)* **L**, **T**, and **W:** no data available.

Plate 15

Plate 16

Plate 17

1♂ +j

2

3

SIMIIFORMES
PLATYRRHINI
Cebidae
Callitrichinae

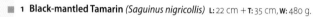

Tamarins

GENUS *Saguinus* | **Tamarins** | 17 species | Plates 18–21

Tamarins in the genus *Saguinus* are distinguished from marmosets primarily by the absence of bands on the tail fur. Furthermore, the head is not adorned with tufts of hair alongside the ears. Some species, such as the Pied Tamarin, in fact have a relatively bare face. The different *Saguinus* species are recognizable primarily by pelage coloration.

■ **1 Black-mantled Tamarin** *(Saguinus nigricollis)* **L:** 22 cm + **T:** 35 cm, **W:** 480 g.

■ **2 Golden-mantled Tamarin** *(Saguinus tripartitus)* **L:** 21–24 cm + **T:** 31–34 cm, **W:** 340 g.

■ **3 Andean Saddleback Tamarin** *(Saguinus fuscicollis leucogenys)* **L:** 22 cm + **T:** 32 cm, **W:** 380–400 g.

■ **3b Saddleback Tamarin** subspecies not illustrated.

■ **4 White-mantled Tamarin** *(Saguinus melanoleucus melanoleucus)* **L:** 22 cm + **T:** 32 cm, **W:** 400 g.

■ **5 Weddell's Tamarin** *(Saguinus fuscicollis weddelli)* **L:** 22 cm + **T:** 32 cm, **W:** 400 g.

SIMIIFORMES

PLATYRRHINI

Cebidae

Callitrichinae

Tamarins

GENUS *Saguinus* | **Tamarins** | 17 species | Plates 18–21

Plate 19

■ **1 White-lipped Tamarin** *(Saguinus labiatus)* **L:** 26 cm + **T:** 39 cm, **W:** 460 g.

■ **2 Midas Tamarin** *(Saguinus midas)* **L:** 24 cm + **T:** 39 cm, **W:** 430 g (female); 586 g (male).

■ **3 Moustached Tamarin** *(Saguinus mystax)* **L:** 26 cm + **T:** 38 cm, **W:** 500–640 g.

■ **4 Black Tamarin** *(Saguinus niger)* **L**, **T**, and **W:** no data available.

Plate 20

■ **1 Pied Tamarin** *(Saguinus bicolor)* **L:** 20–28 cm + **T:** 33–42 cm, **W:** 430 g.

■ **2 Emperor Tamarin** *(Saguinus imperator subgrisescens)* **L:** 23–25 cm + **T:** 39–41 cm, **W:** 450 g.

■ **3 Martins's Tamarin** *(Saguinus martinsi)* **L**, **T**, and **W:** no data available.

■ **4 Mottle-faced Tamarin** *(Saguinus inustus)* **L:** 23 cm + **T:** 36 cm, **W:** 400–500 g.

Plate 21

■ **1 Cotton-top Tamarin** *(Saguinus oedipus)* **L:** 23 cm + **T:** 37 cm, **W:** 410–430 g.

■ **2 Geoffroy's Tamarin** *(Saguinus geoffroyi)* **L:** 25 cm + **T:** 34 cm, **W:** 545 g.

■ **3 White-footed Tamarin** *(Saguinus leucopus)* **L:** 24 cm + **T:** 39 cm, **W:** 440 g.

Plate 19

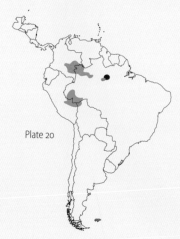

Plate 20

Plate 21

SIMIIFORMES

PLATYRRHINI

Cebidae

Callitrichinae

Lion Tamarins

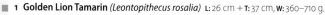

GENUS *Leontopithecus* | **Lion tamarins** | 4 species | Plate 22

Lion tamarins, which are the largest-bodied members of the subfamily Callitrichinae, owe their name to the striking silky fur surrounding the head and shoulders, rather like a lion's mane. In contrast to the other tamarin genera, they do not feed on sap and other exudates. Instead, they essentially depend on insects, which they ferret out beneath tree bark using their long fingers. At nightfall they take refuge in hollows in tree trunks, excavated either naturally or by other animals. As a result of habitat destruction in the now much-reduced tropical forest bordering the eastern coast of Brazil, they are counted among the most endangered primates.

1 **Golden Lion Tamarin** *(Leontopithecus rosalia)* L: 26 cm + T: 37 cm, W: 360–710 g.

2 **Golden-rumped Lion Tamarin** *(Leontopithecus chrysopygus)* L: 29 cm + T: 37 cm, W: 540–690 g.

3 **Golden-headed Lion Tamarin** *(Leontopithecus chrysomelas)* L: 26 cm + T: 37 cm, W: 480–700 g.

4 **Black-faced Lion Tamarin** *(Leontopithecus caissara)* L: 30.5 cm + T: 43 cm, W: 600 g.

SIMIIFORMES

PLATYRRHINI

Cebidae

Cebinae

This subfamily of cebids unites two genera, the medium-sized capuchin monkeys and the distinctly smaller squirrel monkeys. One feature that they share, in addition to various anatomical details, is their very varied diet. They are omnivores.

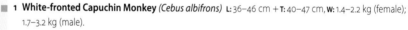

Capuchin Monkeys

GENUS *Cebus* | **Capuchin monkeys** | 12 species | Plate 23

These medium-sized monkeys owe their name to the fact that most species have a small cap of black fur on the head, reminiscent of the tonsure of Capuchin monks. Capuchin monkeys have a robust body covered in thick fur with varied color patterns. Their rounded faces are quite familiar, because these monkeys have long been sold as companion animals and trained for human entertainment. They have a prehensile tail, with smooth skin on the underside of the tip. This hairless zone functions like a fifth hand, permitting capuchin monkeys to suspend themselves from branches, anchored solidly, and liberating their two hands to manipulate food and other objects. They are highly social, living in groups of twenty to thirty individuals and communicating with one another by means of a quite variable range of calls. From birth onward, the infant climbs onto its mother's back, and males may also carry it around. Black-capped Capuchin Monkeys (*Cebus apella*) have the largest geographical distribution among the New World monkeys of South America. They have also been studied most by primatologists, both in the field and in the laboratory. Capuchin monkeys are found in all rain forests, in secondary forests, in mangroves, and also in dry forests. They have a very varied diet, even including crabs and oysters. They possess remarkable cognitive capacities, notably in using tools, similar to chimpanzees.

■ 1 **White-fronted Capuchin Monkey** (*Cebus albifrons*) **L:** 36–46 cm + **T:** 40–47 cm, **W:** 1.4–2.2 kg (female); 1.7–3.2 kg (male).

■ 2 **Black-capped Capuchin Monkey** (*Cebus apella*) **L:** 35–49 cm + **T:** 37–49 cm, **W:** 1.4–3.4 kg (female); 1.3–4.8 kg (male).

■ 3 **Golden-bellied Capuchin Monkey** (*Cebus xanthosternos*) **L:** 36–42 cm + **T:** 38–49 cm, **W:** 1.4–3.4 kg (female); 1.3–4.8 kg (male).

■ 4 **White-faced Capuchin Monkey** (*Cebus capucinus*) **L:** 33–45 cm + **T:** 35–51 cm, **W:** 3.8 kg.

SIMIIFORMES

PLATYRRHINI

Cebidae

Cebinae

Squirrel Monkeys

GENUS *Saimiri* | **Squirrel monkeys** | 5 species | Plate 24

No squirrels live in the tropical forests of South and Central America. Instead, in terms of size, appearance, and patterns of locomotion, squirrel monkeys—along with marmosets and tamarins—occupy this vacant ecological niche. In contrast to many other New World monkeys, with the notable exception of marmosets and tamarins, squirrel monkeys have a prehensile tail only when very young. As they grow up, they lose the capacity to use their tail like a hand. Being small and particularly appealing, countless squirrel monkeys have been captured to supply the trade in companion animals. But they have also been widely used for experiments in medical and pharmaceutical laboratories. They are highly social, living in groups of some twenty to forty individuals, including several males as well as several females. They often share trees with capuchin monkeys and uakaris (*Cacajao*). Squirrel monkeys are very adept, using their hands to forage for the insects, small crabs, snails, and even frogs on which they feed.

1 Black-capped Squirrel Monkey *(Saimiri boliviensis peruviensis)* L: 31 cm + T: 36 cm, W: 700–900 g (female); 960 g–1.1 kg (male).

2 Common Squirrel Monkey *(Saimiri sciureus sciureus)* L: 31 cm + T: 40 cm, W: 550 g–1.2 kg.

3 Black Squirrel Monkey *(Saimiri vanzolinii)* L: 27–32 cm + T: 41–44 cm, W: 650–950 g.

4 Colombian Common Squirrel Monkey *(Saimiri sciureus albigena)* L: 31 cm + T: 40 cm, W: 550 g–1.2 kg.

5 Squirrel monkey species not illustrated.

SIMIIFORMES

PLATYRRHINI

Nyctipithecidae

Aotinae

This subfamily contains the only nocturnal primates in the New World, allocated to the single genus *Aotus*.

Owl Monkeys

GENUS *Aotus* | **Owl monkeys** | 8 species | Plate 25

These species, also called douroucoulis or night monkeys, are more widely known as "owl monkeys" because of their loud vocalizations closely resembling the hoots of those big night-hunting raptors. In contrast to nocturnal lemurs and lorises, the eyes of *Aotus* species do not have a specialized membrane (*tapetum lucidum*) to reflect light rays back through the retina. Instead, they have very large, globular eyes to permit good vision during the night. Their very dense, woolly pelage is mainly silvery gray, with a lighter fawn color on the belly. The head is decorated with three black stripes bordered with gray, emphasizing the upper margins of the eyes. The ears are small and buried in the fur. Owl monkeys are monogamous, living in pairs and accompanied by their maturing offspring. They inhabit tropical forests, occupying territories of about eight acres, marking the boundaries with a scent gland located at the root of the nonprehensile tail. They feed mainly on fruits, leaves, and insects, and spend the daytime either in tree trunk cavities excavated by other species or in tangles of lianas, where predators are unable to reach them.

■ **1 Three-striped Owl Monkey** *(Aotus trivirgatus)* **L:** 34 cm + **T:** 35–37 cm, **W:** 920–950 g.

■ **2 Black-headed Owl Monkey** *(Aotus nigriceps)* **L:** 34 cm + **T:** 36 cm, **W:** 700 g–1.1 kg.

■ **3 Gray-bellied Owl Monkey** *(Aotus lemurinus)* **L:** about 35 cm + **T:** 35 cm, **W:** up to 1 kg.

INFRAORDER	**SIMIIFORMES**
PARVORDER	**PLATYRRHINI**
FAMILY	**Atelidae**

This family contains woolly monkeys, spider monkeys, woolly spider monkeys, and howler monkeys.

SUBFAMILY	**Atelinae**

The genera *Lagothrix*, *Brachyteles*, *Ateles*, and *Alouatta* are allocated to this subfamily.

Woolly Monkeys and Spider Monkeys

GENUS *Lagothrix* | **Woolly monkeys** | 2 species | Plate 26

Woolly monkeys have the densest hair of all primates. Although they seem rather plump for animals living exclusively in the upper levels of flooded and montane tropical rain forests, they are nevertheless extremely agile. Using their prehensile tail like a fifth hand permits them to perform all kinds of acrobatics. Their diet is made up of items from more than two hundred plant species, and they play a prominent part in the dispersal of the seeds of the fruits they ingest. They are very vulnerable to habitat destruction and are counted among the most endangered primate species. Woolly monkeys are social, living in groups usually containing about thirty individuals and sometimes as many as seventy, including several males and females accompanied by their maturing offspring. Within a group there is a strong hierarchical relationship among the males, essentially linked to individual age. The dominant male behaves very protectively toward females and toward their infants during the first two months of life. During the first week after birth, the mother carries her infant on her belly, but it later moves to her back, where it is transported until it reaches the age of about two years.

GENUS *Brachyteles* | **Woolly spider monkeys** | 2 species | Plate 26

Woolly spider monkeys, also known as *muriquis*, are the largest extant New World monkeys. They are particularly threatened because they are restricted to a small zone of very degraded and fragmented tropical forest on the Atlantic coast of Brazil, where lion tamarins are also found. Woolly spider monkeys live in quite flexible groups containing about twenty individuals, showing a so-called fission-fusion structure: A group regularly splits into small subgroups that may reunite some time later. They spend a large part of the day foraging for food (leaves, fruits, seeds, nectar) and engaging in social interactions. They are among the least aggressive primates and are often observed wrapping their arms around each other for reassurance. This has earned them the label "hippy monkeys."

1 **Humboldt's Woolly Monkey** *(Lagothrix lagotricha lagotricha)* L: 49–52 cm + T: 67 cm, W: 3.5–6.5 kg (female); 3.6–10 kg (male).

2 **Colombian Woolly Monkey** *(Lagothrix lagotricha lugens)* L: 49–52 cm + T: 67 cm, W: 3.5–6.5 kg (female); 3.6–10 kg (male).

3 **Poeppig's Woolly Monkey** *(Lagothrix lagotricha poeppigii)* L: 49–52 cm + T: 67 cm, W: 3.5–6.5 kg (female); 3.6–10 kg (male).

4 **Gray Woolly Monkey** *(Lagothrix lagotricha cana)* L: 49–52 cm + T: 67 cm, W: 3.5–6.5 kg (female); 3.6–10 kg (male).

5 **Yellow-tailed Woolly Monkey** *(Lagothrix flavicauda)* L: 51–53 cm + T: 56–61 cm, W: 10 kg.

6 **Northern Woolly Spider Monkey** *(Brachyteles hypoxanthus)* L: 50–78 cm + T: 79 cm, W: 9.5–11 kg (female); 12–15 kg (male).

7 **Southern Woolly Spider Monkey** *(Brachyteles arachnoides)* L: 57–59 cm + T: 79 cm, W: 9.4 kg (female); 12 kg (male).

SIMIIFORMES
PLATYRRHINI
Atelidae
Atelinae

Spider Monkeys

GENUS *Ateles* | **Spider monkeys** | 7 species | Plate 27

Slender and gracile, spider monkeys have very long fore and hind limbs in addition to a long tail. The hairless undersurface at the tip of the tail bears skin ridges, like the fingerprints on the hands and feet, and the tail functions like a fifth hand. Spider monkeys are highly specialized for an acrobatic lifestyle in the upper levels of the tropical rain forest. The thumbs have been reduced to the extent that they seem to have been lost. This has transformed their hands into veritable hooks, permitting them to hang beneath branches and to swing from one tree to another with astonishing dexterity. They spend a great deal of time feeding on leaves and fruits, occasionally ingesting dead wood and soil as well. Spider monkeys live in social groups with a fission-fusion structure, containing some twenty individuals. Members generally spend the daytime in small subgroups of three to four individuals but reunite regularly in the core of their territory, extending over 250 to 750 acres, which they fiercely defend against predators and intruders. Females possess a very long clitoris, which they use to scent mark their territorial boundaries. These primates have a notably large brain relative to body size and are highly intelligent. The female gives birth to a single infant every three years, following a gestation lasting about seven and a half months. A young spider monkey takes about six years to become adult and independent.

■ **1 White-fronted Spider Monkey** *(Ateles belzebuth)* L: 41–58 cm + T: 68–90 cm, W: 7.2–10 kg.

■ **2 Geoffroy's Spider Monkey** *(Ateles geoffroyi)* L: 30–63 cm + T: 63–84 cm, W: 6–9 kg.

■ **3 Red-faced Spider Monkey** *(Ateles paniscus)* L: 54 cm + T: 81 cm, W: 5.4–11 kg.

■ **4 White-cheeked Spider Monkey** *(Ateles marginatus)* L: 34–50 cm + T: 61–77 cm, W: 5.8 kg.

■ **5 Peruvian Spider Monkey** *(Ateles chamek)* L: 40–52 cm + T: 80–88 cm, W: 7 kg.

■ **6 Brown-headed Spider Monkey** *(Ateles fusciceps robustus)* L: 39–53 cm + T: 71–85 cm, W: 8.8 kg.

SIMIIFORMES

PLATYRRHINI

Atelidae

Atelinae

Howler Monkeys

GENUS *Alouatta* | **Howler monkeys** | 9 species | Plate 28

Howler monkeys owe their name to their powerful calls, which they are able to generate thanks to a special development of the hyoid bone, located close to the larynx. Their hyoid has become a hollow capsule that serves as a resonator. Males and females "howl" to advertise the limits of the group's territory to potential intruders. Howling is most frequent around midday or in the late afternoon, but may also occur at dawn or during a full moon. Howler monkeys are unique among New World monkeys in that their diet, in addition to fruits, flowers, and young leaves, includes mature leaves, which are difficult to digest and very poor in energy yield. So they are obliged to eat a large quantity of food every day, more than two pounds, to obtain sufficient energy to meet their requirements. In order to avoid excessive energy expenditure, they are relatively inactive and spend considerable time resting. Howler monkeys live in small social groups typically containing about five individuals, including several males and females. They live in a variety of tropical forest habitats, ranging from mangroves through lowland rain forests to wooded savannas. The sexes are dimorphic, the females smaller than the males. In the Black Howler Monkey, the sexes are also distinguished by the color of the pelage; males are ebony-colored, while females are yellowish brown.

- **1 Bolivian Red Howler Monkey** *(Alouatta sara)* **L:** 54 cm + **T:** 59 cm, **w:** about 5 kg (female); 7 kg (male).
- **2 Venezuelan Red Howler Monkey** *(Alouatta seniculus)* **L:** 52–58 cm + **T:** 60 cm, **w:** 4.2–7 kg (female); 5.4–9 kg (male).
- **3 Mantled Howler Monkey** *(Alouatta palliata)* **L:** 52–56 cm + **T:** 60 cm, **w:** 3.1–7.6 kg (female); 4.5–9.8 kg (male).
- **4 Black Howler Monkey** *(Alouatta caraya)* **L:** 42–55 cm + **T:** 53–65 cm, **w:** 3.8–5.4 kg (female); 5–8.3 kg (male).

INFRAORDER

PARVORDER

FAMILY

SIMIIFORMES

PLATYRRHINI

Pitheciidae

The family Pitheciidae contains four genera, uniting saki monkeys, bearded sakis, uakaris, and titi monkeys. These are certainly the strangest primates with respect to appearance. No member of this family possesses a prehensile tail. They all have very specialized incisors and canines, which they use to open and crush the seeds that make up a prominent part of their diets.

SUBFAMILY

Pitheciinae

This subfamily includes the sakis and uakaris, medium-sized primates with a strange appearance and unusual face.

Saki Monkeys

GENUS *Pithecia* | **Saki monkeys** | 5 species | Plate 29

In all of these monkeys, the fur on the head has a striking appearance. Moreover, the pelage is different colored in males and females. In the White-faced Saki Monkey, the male's fur is completely black, apart from the white facial mask, whereas the female is uniformly gray, with her nose framed by two little stripes of white fur. At birth, all infants have the same pelage color as females. Monk Saki Monkeys live in small family groups, usually occupying the upper strata of the forest but sometimes descending into bushes. Sakis feed predominantly on fruits and seeds, although their diet also includes leaves, flowers, and various animal prey species, in addition to iron-rich soil from termite mounds. They are capable of performing impressive leaps, of rapid running along branches with arms raised, and of hanging by their feet. Their powerful calls serve to stake out the boundaries of their territories, which range in size from ten to twenty-five acres.

1 **Buffy Saki Monkey** *(Pithecia pithecia)* L: 34 cm + T: 34–39 cm, W: 780 g–1.7 kg (female); 960 g–2.5 kg (male).

2 **Monk Saki Monkey** *(Pithecia monachus)* L: 37–48 cm + T: 40–50 cm, W: 1.3–2.5 kg (female); 2.5–3.1 kg (male).

3 **Rio Tapajós Saki Monkey** *(Pithecia irrorata)* L: 37–42 cm + T: 47–54 cm, W: 2.1 kg (female); 2.9 kg (male).

4 **White-footed Saki Monkey** *(Pithecia albicans)* L: 38 cm + T: 41 cm, W: 3 kg.

SIMIIFORMES

PLATYRRHINI

Pitheciidae

Pitheciinae

Uakaris and Bearded Saki Monkeys

GENUS *Cacajao* | **Uakaris** | 3 species | Plate 30

Bald-faced uakaris, with their completely hairless, scarlet heads, have a particularly arresting appearance. By contrast, the Black-headed Uakari has a crown of hair. The tail is greatly reduced in all uakaris, and all have a long, hairy "cape," which may be reddish brown or black, or even completely white in certain bald-faced uakaris. Uakaris live in groups of fifteen to thirty individuals, containing several males and females. They occur along small rivers inside swampy and flooded forests, moving around in the crowns of tall trees. When disturbed, uakaris flick their tails repeatedly and, if the threat persists, may utter powerful, high-pitched alarm calls. In addition to some ten vocalizations, uakaris use facial expressions to communicate with one another.

GENUS *Chiropotes* | **Bearded saki monkeys** | 2 species | Plate 30

Bearded saki monkeys, which owe their name to a well-developed clump of hair on the chin, live in small groups of five to ten individuals in lowland and montane tropical rain forests. They feed on seeds, fruits, and flowers. Following a five-month gestation, the female gives birth to a single infant with a prehensile tail that it uses to cling to its mother's fur. This ability to use the tail like a fifth hand fades as the infant grows.

- **1 White Bald-faced Uakari** *(Cacajao calvus calvus)* **L:** 55 cm + **T:** 15.5 cm, **W:** 2.8 kg (female); 3.4 kg (male).
- **2 Red Bald-faced Uakari** *(Cacajao calvus rubicundus)* **L:** 55 cm + **T:** 15.5 cm, **W:** 2.8 kg (female); 3.4 kg (male).
- **3 Black-headed Uakari** *(Cacajao melanocephalus)* **L:** 30–50 cm + **T:** 12–21 cm, **W:** 2.4–4 kg.
- **4 Red-backed Bearded Saki Monkey** *(Chiropotes chiropotes)* **L:** 40–42 cm + **T:** 39 cm, **W:** 1.9–3.3 kg (female); 2.2–4 kg (male).
- **4b Black-bearded Saki Monkey**: species not illustrated.
- **5 White-nosed Saki Monkey** *(Chiropotes albinasus)* **L:** 42 cm + **T:** 41 cm, **W:** 2.2–3.3 kg.

SIMIIFORMES

PLATYRRHINI

Pitheciidae

Callicebinae

This subfamily contains the small-bodied titi monkeys, all allocated to the single genus *Callicebus*.

Titi Monkeys

GENUS *Callicebus* | **Titi monkeys** | 29 species | Plate 31

The diminutive titi monkeys live in tightly bonded pairs. It is common to see a male and female sitting close to one another on a branch, with their elongated, bushy tails—covered with long, soft hairs—coiled around each other. They inhabit various kinds of forests, ranging from lowland to montane and including swampy regions. Their territories, extending over fifteen to thirty acres, are often shared with tamarins, marmosets, and even woolly monkeys. Every morning, the titi pair sings a duet, which serves both to deter intruders and to strengthen the pair bond. In titi monkeys, it is usually the male that carries the infant, particularly during the first weeks after birth. Although titi monkeys have pelage patterns that provide good camouflage, their slow, cautious movement through the trees plays a greater role in preventing predators from detecting them. Titis feed mainly on fruits and leaves but also prey on insects and spiders.

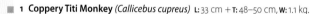

■ **1 Coppery Titi Monkey** (*Callicebus cupreus*) **L:** 33 cm + **T:** 48–50 cm, **W:** 1.1 kg.

■ **2 Atlantic Titi Monkey** (*Callicebus personatus*) **L:** 35–38 cm + **T:** 42 cm, **W:** 1.2–1.3 kg.

■ **3 White-eared Titi Monkey** (*Callicebus donacophilus*) **L:** 31–34 cm + **T:** 41–44 cm, **W:** 800 g.

■ **4 Collared Titi Monkey** (*Callicebus torquatus*) **L:** 32 cm + **T:** 39–41 cm, **W:** 1.1–1.5 kg.

■ **5 Brown Titi Monkey** (*Callicebus brunneus*) **L:** 31cm + **T:** 39–41 cm, **W:** 845–850 g.

TARSIIFORMES

Tarsiidae

Tarsiers constitute a special group among primates, because they share some characteristics with lemurs and others with higher primates. This is why investigators have classified them in their own infraorder containing only the single extant genus *Tarsius*. However, various related fossil forms, allocated to a score of different genera, have been found in North America and Western Europe, dating back between thirty-six and fifty-four million years. Today, tarsiers live exclusively in the tropical forests of Southeast Asia, in the Philippines, Borneo, Sulawesi (formerly Celebes), and Sumatra. They owe their name to the particular form of the tarsus (ankle region) of the hind limb. The tarsal bones are markedly elongated and function rather like a spring, permitting extensive leaps from tree to tree—from four feet to more than fifteen feet on occasions.

Tarsiers

GENUS *Tarsius* | **Tarsiers** | 7 species | Plate 32

Tarsiers are nocturnal and possess a round, very mobile head that can be rotated through more than 180 degrees. Moreover, they have particularly large, globular eyes and very large ears. This combination allows them to find their way around without difficulty after nightfall and to capture—using their hands—the various invertebrates and small reptiles on which they feed. To move around, they leap from branch to branch with a vertical posture. Their agility while moving is due not only to the special configuration of the ankle bones but also to the small adhesive pads on their digits and the long, thin tail, used to balance the body. Swift movement and the neutral color of the pelage, ranging from gray to ochre, protect them from many predators. Tarsiers live in relatively stable pairs, accompanied by their maturing offspring, occupying forest territories of two and a half to seven and a half acres and marking the boundaries using urine and a secretion produce by a gland on the chest. During territorial conflicts, they utter powerful, high-pitched calls. Mating takes place between October and December, and gestation lasts six months, which is exceptionally long for such a small animal. When the infant is born, between April and June, it is already able to move around in the environment. However, it takes about a month before it can perform real leaps like adults. Tarsiers can live for more than ten years.

■ **1 Horsfield's Tarsier** *(Tarsius bancanus)* **L:** about 13 cm + **T:** 22 cm, **W:** 110 g (female); 120 g (male).

■ **2 Philippine Tarsier** *(Tarsius syrichta)* **L:** about 12 cm + **T:** 23 cm, **W:** 120 g (female); 130 g (male).

■ **3 Spectral Tarsier** *(Tarsius spectrum)* **L:** 12 cm + **T:** 24 cm, **W:** 110 g (female); 120 g (male).

LORISIFORMES

LORISOIDEA

Lorisidae

The superfamily Lorisoidea is divided into two families: Lorisidae, containing some species that occur in Asia and others in Africa, and Galagidae, which contains uniquely African primates (see Plates 51 and 52). Asian lorises, which are all nocturnal, solitary, and small to medium-sized, are found in many tropical and subtropical forests. They do not leap but rather move around in the trees quite slowly and discreetly to escape the attention of predators. The tail is either very reduced or completely lacking. Lorises firmly grasp the substrate as they move around: Their hands form veritable pincers, thanks to reduction of the second finger, and their feet, which have opposable big toes, are also highly prehensile. Moreover, a blood-retention system permits prolonged oxygen supply to the limb muscles without cramping, allowing them to remain contracted for extended periods without tiring. Lorises feed on fruits, sap, insects, and small vertebrates that they are able to catch in the foliage because of their good sight and hearing.

Lorises

GENUS *Nycticebus* | **Slow lorises** | 3 species | Plate 33

In both physical appearance and behavior, slow lorises closely resemble African pottos. Despite the great geographical separation between them, they probably shared a common origin. The same is true of slender lorises and African angwantibos.

Slow lorises have a life expectancy of some twenty years. Females give birth every twelve to eighteen months to a single infant after a gestation of about six months. At birth, the infants are silvery gray, but their long, silky fur fades away after about eleven weeks. When the mother sets out to forage for food, she hides her infant in a cavity of some kind, such as a tree hollow, and returns to retrieve it as soon as she has finished feeding.

GENUS *Loris* | **Slender lorises** | 2 species | Plate 33

Slender lorises, endowed with very thin, elongated limbs and a particularly strange and lanky appearance, clearly deserve their name. Like other lorises, they are nocturnal and possess both excellent vision and exceptionally good hearing. During the daytime, they sleep in trees, huddled closely together in small groups of two to four individuals. Slender lorises rarely descend to the ground. They feed predominantly on insects, rounding off their diet with a few fruits, flowers, leaves, eggs and small vertebrates. The female gives birth to one or two infants after a gestation of five months. When slender lorises are frightened, they emit a foul-smelling odor originating from a gland located close to the hind limbs.

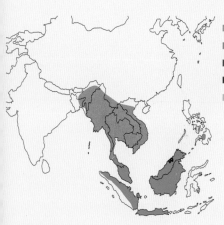

■ 1 **Bengal Slow Loris** *(Nycticebus bengalensis)* **L**, **T**, and **w**: no data available.

■ 2 **Common Slow Loris** *(Nycticebus coucang)* **L**: about 30 cm + **T**: 2 cm, **w**: 600 g–1 kg.

■ 3 **Pygmy Slow Loris** *(Nycticebus pygmaeus)* **L**: 25 cm, **w**: about 400 g.

■ 4 **Common Slender Loris** *(Loris tardigradus)* **L**: about 20 cm + **T**: 1 cm, **w**: 300 g.

■ 5 **Lydekker's Slender Loris** *(Loris lydekkerianus)* **L**: about 20 cm + **T**: 1 cm, **w**: 300 g.

SIMIIFORMES

CATARRHINI

CERCOPITHECOIDEA

Cercopithecidae

Old World monkeys make up a very large family containing about one hundred species allocated to twenty-one genera. They are found in many different regions of Africa, in the south
of the Arabian Peninsula, Southern and Central Asia, and Japan. They are divided into two
subfamilies on the basis of dietary habits: Cercopithecinae and Colobinae.

Cercopithecinae

Cercopithecines are also called "cheek-pouched monkeys" because they have sacs in their
cheeks in which they can store large amounts of food that they subsequently masticate
little by little over the course of the day. All of these monkeys are diurnal and predominantly
tree living, although—in contrast to other primates—they can easily adapt to terrestrial
life. Indeed, some species, such as macaques, often spend time on the ground. They are
characterized by a relatively stocky body with the forelimbs generally shorter than the hind
limbs. On the hand, the thumb is well developed. The tail is variable in length and sometimes
markedly reduced or absent, but, in contrast to many South American monkeys, the tail is
never prehensile.

Macaques

GENUS *Macaca* | **Macaques** | 22 species | Plates 34–37

Macaques are stockier than other cheek-pouched monkeys. The snout is more prominent,
but the nostrils do not reach the upper lip. Differences between species are very limited and
mainly involve details of pelage coloration. Only a few species stand out from the others,
such as the Lion-tailed Macaque with its striking mane and the macaques living on the
Sulawesi archipelago (Tonkean Macaque, Crested Black Macaque, etc.). With the sole exception of the Barbary Macaque of North Africa (Plate 64), all live in Asia, displaying an extensive
geographical distribution in Southeast Asia, India, eastern Tibet, China, Sri Lanka, and Japan.

Macaques colonize diverse habitats, including both tropical rain forests and dry forests.
Tibetan and Japanese macaques, the northernmost primates, can even be found in mountainous areas up to an elevation of 6,000 feet. Some have even invaded towns, notably in
Thailand. In winter, some Japanese macaques have been observed making snowballs solely
for play. Others, regularly fed by local inhabitants, bathe in natural sources of hot water, and a
small population in southern Japan has become famous for washing food in seawater. In that
case, scientists speak of tradition, or even culture, because such washing behavior, pioneered
by a female in the 1960s, has been transmitted from generation to generation down to the
present day. All macaques are diurnal and essentially frugivorous, although they have a great
capacity for adaptation. They can live on all kinds of foods: leaves, buds, insects, eggs, small
vertebrates, crustaceans. Some raid human crops or pick through trash containers in the
towns where they live. They readily climb trees but are also at home on the ground, where
they often move around. *(Description continued on p. 112)*

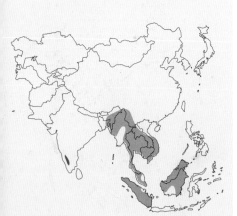

■ **1 Pig-tailed Macaque** *(Macaca nemestrina)* **L:** 46–56 cm + **T:** 13–24 cm, **W:** 5 kg (female); 15 kg (male).

■ **2 Pagai Island Macaque** *(Macaca pagensis)* **L:** 46–56 cm + **T:** 13–24 cm, **W:** 5 kg (female); 15 kg (male).

■ **3 Lion-tailed Macaque** *(Macaca silenus)* **L:** 46–61 cm + **T:** 25–38 cm, **W:** 4.5 kg (female); 7–8 kg (male).

1♂

1♀ +j

2

3

3

SIMIIFORMES

CATARRHINI

CERCOPITHECOIDEA

Cercopithecidae

Cercopithecinae

Macaques

GENUS *Macaca* | **Macaques** | 22 species | Plates 34–37

(Description continued from p. 110)

In some species, when females become sexually receptive, the skin in the anogenital region becomes bright red in color, signaling readiness to copulate to males. The degree of development of this signal varies among the species. As a general rule, a female macaque will give birth to a single infant after a gestation period of about five and a half months. Macaques are highly social and live in large groups usually containing several males and females, with more-or-less strict hierarchies between individuals of the same sex. Macaques are the primates most used in biomedical research, particularly Rhesus Macaques, which gave their name to the Rhesus factors in blood groups. The life expectancy of macaques is about thirty years.

- **1 Tonkean Macaque** *(Macaca tonkeana)* **L:** 50–67 cm + **T:** 2.8–7 cm, **W:** 8.6–10 kg.
- **2 Crested Black Macaque** *(Macaca nigra)* **L:** 44–57 cm + **T:** 2.5 cm, **W:** 5.5 kg (female); 9 kg (male).
- **3 Moor Macaque** *(Macaca maura)* **L:** 50–69 cm + **T:** 4 cm, **W:** no data available.
- **4 Booted Macaque** *(Macaca ochreata)* **L:** 50–59 cm + **T:** 3.5–4 cm, **W:** no data available.
- **5 Heck's Macaque** *(Macaca hecki)* **L:** 42–66 cm + **T:** 1.5–4 cm, **W:** no data available.

1 ♂

3

2 ♂

4

5

2 ♀ +j

2 ♂

Macaques

GENUS *Macaca* | **Macaques** | 22 species | Plates 34–37

■ **1 Long-tailed Macaque** *(Macaca fascicularis)* **L:** 38–64 cm + **T:** 4–5.5 cm, **W:** 4 kg (female); 7 kg (male).

■ **2 Formosan Rock Macaque** *(Macaca cyclopis)* **L:** 40–55 cm + **T:** 2.6–5 cm, **W:** 5 kg (female); 6 kg (male).

■ **3 Japanese Macaque** *(Macaca fuscata)* **L:** 47–60 cm + **T:** 7–12 cm, **W:** 8 kg (female); 12 kg (male).

■ **4 Rhesus Macaque** *(Macaca mulatta)* **L:** 47–63 cm + **T:** 18–30 cm, **W:** 5 kg (female); 7.5 kg (male).

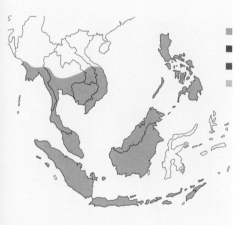

SIMIIFORMES
CATARRHINI
CERCOPITHECOIDEA
Cercopithecidae
Cercopithecinae

Macaques

GENUS *Macaca* | **Macaques** | 22 species | Plates 34–37

1 **Tibetan Macaque** *(Macaca thibetana)* **L:** 50–71 cm + **T:** 5.5–8 cm, **W:** 13 kg (female); 16 kg (male).

2 **Bonnet Macaque** *(Macaca radiata)* **L:** 37–59 cm + **T:** 33–60 cm, **W:** 4 kg (female); 7 kg (male).

3 **Stump-tailed Macaque** *(Macaca arctoides)* **L:** 48–65 cm + **T:** 1.5–7 cm, **W:** 8 kg (female); 10 kg (male).

4 **Assam Macaque** *(Macaca assamensis)* **L:** 43–73 cm + **T:** 20–29 cm, **W:** 7 kg (female); 12 kg (male).

5 **Toque Macaque** *(Macaca sinica)* **L:** 43–53 cm + **T:** 46–60 cm, **W:** 4 kg (female); 6–8 kg (male).

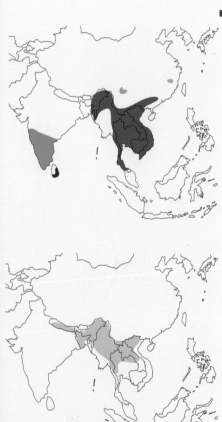

1♀ +j

1♂

2♂

3♂

3 j

4♂

5♂

INFRAORDER

PARVORDER

SUPERFAMILY

FAMILY

SUBFAMILY

SIMIIFORMES

CATARRHINI

CERCOPITHECOIDEA

Cercopithecidae

Colobinae

Colobines, or leaf monkeys, make up the smaller of the two subfamilies of Old World monkeys, numbering fewer species than the Cercopithecinae. Colobines are graceful monkeys with slender bodies and limbs. They have a long tail, often ending in a tuft, that helps them to maintain balance as they leap from tree to tree like agile trapeze artists. They live in social groups ranging in size from ten to more than one hundred individuals, containing one or several males and numerous females accompanied by their offspring. They devote a large part of their time to social relationships, especially grooming sessions that serve to strengthen the bonds between individuals. Colobine monkeys feed almost exclusively on leaves, which are difficult to digest because of their high cellulose content. Like cows, leaf monkeys have a complex stomach divided into several compartments, some of which house colonies of bacteria that are specialized for degradation and digestion of the cellulose in leaves. Because this food source is poor in nutrients, very large quantities must be ingested. Moreover, as fermentation of the leaves generates gas, the stomach is often swollen and distended in colobine monkeys.

Southern Odd-nosed Monkeys

GENUS *Nasalis* | **Southern odd-nosed monkeys** | 2 species | Plate 38

Although they are allocated to the same genus, *Nasalis*, the Proboscis Monkey and the Pig-tailed Langur are distinguished not only by pelage color and body weight (the Proboscis Monkey being twice as heavy as the Pig-tailed Langur) but also, most strikingly, by the shape of the nose. Whereas the Pig-tailed Langur has a small snub nose, the nose of the Proboscis Monkey is large and bulging, especially in the male, hence the name given to the species. Thanks to the particularly large resonance chamber in the nose, calls emitted by the male resemble loud honks, while the female's calls are rather goose-like. The Pig-tailed Langur is more discreet, but males nevertheless engage in dialogues using powerful nasal vocalizations. Both Proboscis Monkeys and Pig-tailed Langurs live in groups containing about ten individuals, mostly including a single male and several females. Groups of bachelor males are also encountered. These leaf monkeys live in home ranges covering about three and a half square miles and are not territorial. Different groups can meet up and even feed in the same tree. Although these monkeys primarily eat leaves, their diets also include fruits and seeds, particularly between January and May, in the case of Proboscis Monkeys. Just four plant species provide the bulk of their diet. These primates are extremely vulnerable to any disturbance of their habitat, especially deforestation. Both species of southern odd-nosed monkeys inhabit primary swamp forests, and Proboscis Monkeys, which are excellent swimmers, also live in mangroves.

1 **Proboscis Monkey** *(Nasalis larvatus)* **L:** 62–75 cm + **T:** 60 cm, **W:** 10–20 kg.

2 **Pig-tailed Langur** *(Nasalis concolor)* **L:** 50 cm + **T:** 15 cm, **W:** 7–8.7 kg.

2

1♂

1♂

1j

1♀

SIMIIFORMES

CATARRHINI

CERCOPITHECOIDEA

Cercopithecidae

Colobinae

Douc Langurs

GENUS *Pygathrix* | **Douc langurs** | 3 species | Plate 39

Douc langurs have an unusually colorful pelage: gray back and belly; black thighs, hands, feet, and forehead; brown legs; and white cheeks, throat, tail, and forearms. This striking pelage pattern is rounded off with an ochre face decorated with a white nose and pale blue eyelids. Because this colorful pelage pattern draws the attention of fur traffickers, all three douc langur species are particularly threatened. They are also a sought-after source of bushmeat.

These agile primates occupy the crowns of trees in tropical forests, where they feed on some fifty plant species. They live in multimale-multifemale groups, with a separate social hierarchy for each sex, although males are generally dominant over females. After a gestation of six months, the female gives birth to a single infant with gray fur and a black face. After a few weeks, this infantile coloration gradually disappears, giving way to the adult pattern. Births take place between January and May, during the period when fruits are most abundant.

- **1 Gray-shanked Douc Langur** *(Pygathrix cinerea)* **L:** 60 cm + **T:** 59–68 cm, **W:** 8–10 kg.
- **2 Red-shanked Douc Langur** *(Pygathrix nemaeus)* **L:** 60 cm + **T:** 56–76 cm, **W:** no data available.
- **3 Black-shanked Douc Langur** *(Pygathrix nigripes)* **L:** 60–76 cm + **T:** 56–76 cm, **W:** no data available.

SIMIIFORMES
CATARRHINI
CERCOPITHECOIDEA
Cercopithecidae
Colobinae

Snub-nosed Monkeys

GENUS *Rhinopithecus* | **Snub-nosed monkeys** | 4 species | Plate 40

Snub-nosed monkeys are recognizable by their colored faces, short nose with upward-tilted nostrils, and wide, thick-lipped mouth that is often highlighted in pink. Three of the four species possess a dense coat of fur that protects them against the extremely harsh winters in the wooded montane regions of China where they occur at altitudes between 6,000 and 9,000 feet. Only the Tonkin Snub-nosed Monkey, which inhabits Vietnamese forests, lacks the heavy fur coat. Snub-nosed monkeys live in social groups containing a single male and several females accompanied by their offspring. But several groups may associate to form bands comprising more than one hundred individuals. During winter, they spend most of their time foraging for buds and lichens buried under the snow. Over the rest of the year they feed on young leaves, flowers, and fruits.

1 **Black Snub-nosed Monkey** *(Rhinopithecus bieti)* **L:** 74–83 cm + **T:** 51–74 cm, **W:** 9–15 kg.

2 **Gray Snub-nosed Monkey** *(Rhinopithecus brelichi)* **L:** 66 cm + **T:** 55–77 cm, **W:** no data available.

3 **Golden Snub-nosed Monkey** *(Rhinopithecus roxellana)* **L:** 68–76 cm + **T:** 64–72 cm, **W:** 8–25 kg.

4 **Tonkin Snub-nosed Monkey** *(Rhinopithecus avunculus)* **L:** 54–65 cm + **T:** 65–85 cm, **W:** 8.5–14 kg.

1♂

1♀ + j

4

2♂

3

3♀ + j

3♂

SIMIIFORMES

CATARRHINI

CERCOPITHECOIDEA

Cercopithecidae

Colobinae

Gray Langurs

GENUS *Semnopithecus* | **Gray langurs** | 7 species | Plate 41

The genus *Semnopithecus*, closely allied to the genus *Presbytis*, includes the gray langurs, which are larger-bodied leaf monkeys with a gray pelage more-or-less tinted with brown and embellished with golden highlights. The hands, feet, and face are black.

This genus, which once included just a single species, has a vast geographical distribution. It has colonized numerous tropical forest habitats extending up to the foothills of the Himalayas, at elevations of more than 12,000 feet. After humans, this is the primate that has occupied the greatest variety of different habitats. In fact, humans and gray langurs often live side by side, most notably in the city of Jodhpur, India. The gray langur is regarded as a sacred monkey personifying Hanuman, the monkey-god of the Ramayana epic, one of the fundamental texts of the Hindu canon. Accordingly, local people regularly provide offerings.

Gray langurs are social and may live either in harems, composed of a single male and several females accompanied by their offspring, or in large multimale-multifemale groups that may contain more than a hundred individuals. Conflicts between males are intense, and when a new male succeeds in monopolizing a group of females, he may kill all existing offspring so the females become fertile more rapidly. Such infanticide permits a male to sire his own offspring without delay, before a rival displaces him from the dominant position. Births take place throughout the year after five to six months of gestation, but in northern India they predominantly occur during the dry season. Gray langurs are most active in the early morning and late afternoon, spending the middle of the day resting and engaging in intense grooming sessions that strengthen bonds between individuals. These langurs are the most terrestrial of the leaf monkeys. They spend more than 80 percent of their time on the ground, moving around and foraging for food: leaves, fruits, and flowers, supplemented by bark and pinecones in the case of the Nepal gray langur. They occupy territories ranging in size from 125 to more than 2,500 acres.

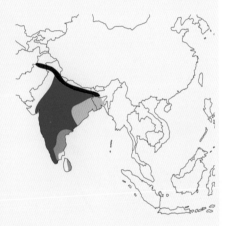

■ **1 Tufted Gray Langur** *(Semnopithecus priam)* L: 40–78 cm + T: 70–97 cm, W: 11–18 kg.

■ **2 Southern Plains Gray Langur** *(Semnopithecus dussumieri)* L: 40–78 cm + T: 70–97 cm, W: 11–18 kg.

■ **3 Northern Plains Gray Langur** *(Semnopithecus entellus)* L: 40–78 cm + T: 70–97 cm, W: 11–18 kg.

■ **4 Nepal Gray Langur** *(Semnopithecus schistaceus)* L: 40–78 cm + T: 70–97 cm, W: 11–18 kg.

SIMIIFORMES

CATARRHINI

CERCOPITHECOIDEA

Cercopithecidae

Colobinae

Lutungs

GENUS *Trachypithecus* | **Lutungs** | 17 species | Plates 42–44

The characteristic skull morphology of these langurs creates the visual impression of raised eyebrows. In addition, they often have a crest on the crown of the head. They are especially adapted for life in the trees. All of them share the peculiarity of giving birth to infants with pelage coloration differing distinctly from that of adults, in most cases having a mandarin-orange hue. It seems that this neonatal pelage (lanugo) serves to neutralize the aggressiveness of males or to trigger affective responses from various members of the social group. The hands, feet, and head gradually become gray or black, and by the age of three months youngsters have the same coloration as adults. These leaf monkeys live in groups generally composed of a single male, several females, and their offspring, occupying territories ranging from 12 to 75 or even 175 acres.

■ 1 **Gee's Golden Langur** *(Trachypithecus geei)* **L:** 49 cm + **T:** 71 cm, **W:** 10 kg.

■ 2 **Capped Langur** *(Trachypithecus pileatus)* **L:** 60 cm + **T:** 85 cm, **W:** 10–12 kg.

■ 3 **Purple-faced Langur** *(Trachypithecus vetulus)* **L:** 48–60 cm + **T:** 66–85 cm, **W:** 5–9 kg.

■ 4 **Nilgiri Langur** *(Trachypithecus johnii)* **L:** 57 cm + **T:** 86 cm, **W:** 10–12 kg.

SIMIIFORMES
CATARRHINI
CERCOPITHECOIDEA
Cercopithecidae
Colobinae

Lutungs

GENUS *Trachypithecus* | **Lutungs** | 17 species | Plates 42–44

■ **1 Hatinh Langur** *(Trachypithecus hatinhensis)* L: 47–64 cm + T: 75–96 cm, W: 5.5–7 kg.

■ **2 François's Langur** *(Trachypithecus francoisi)* L: 54–57 cm + T: 85 cm, W: 5.9 kg.

■ **3 Delacour's Langur** *(Trachypithecus delacouri)* L: 55–83 cm + T: 85 cm, W: 6–10 kg.

■ **4 White-headed Langur** *(Trachypithecus poliocephalus leucocephalus)* L: 47–62 cm + T: 77–89 cm, W: 7–9 kg.

■ **5 Gray-headed Langur** *(Trachypithecus poliocephalus poliocephalus)* L: 47–62 cm + T: 77–89 cm, W: 7–9 kg.

■ **6 Dusky Leaf Monkey** *(Trachypithecus obscurus)* L: 42–67 cm + T: 72 cm, W: 6.6–7 kg.

■ **7 Phayre's Leaf Monkey** *(Trachypithecus phayrei)* L: 51–55 cm + T: 77 cm, W: 6.9–7.9 kg.

Lutungs

GENUS *Trachypithecus* | **Lutungs** | 17 species | Plates 42–44

■ **1 Silvered Leaf Monkey** *(Trachypithecus cristatus)* **L:** 48–54 cm + **T:** 70 cm, **W:** 5.7–6.6 kg.

■ **2 Javan Lutung, black and rufous-brown forms** *(Trachypithecus auratus)* **L:** 46–75 cm + **T:** 61–82 cm, **W:** 7 kg.

SIMIIFORMES
CATARRHINI
CERCOPITHECOIDEA
Cercopithecidae
Colobinae

Surilis

GENUS *Presbytis* | **Surilis** | 11 species | Plate 45

Like other colobine monkeys, langurs of the genus *Presbytis*, known as surilis, feed predominantly on leaves. They are inhabitants of the Malay Peninsula and Indonesia. These primates have relatively long arms and legs, adapted for an acrobatic life in the crowns of trees. They all have a head crest that is developed to varying extents. At birth, infants are generally covered in white fur embellished with a black stripe on the back. This neonatal hair is referred to as the "lanugo." As the infant grows, its pelage slowly changes to acquire the adult coloration.

- **1 Ferruginous Mitered Langur** *(Presbytis melalophos nobilis)* **L:** 50 cm + **T:** 71 cm, **W:** about 6 kg.
- **2 Southern Mitered Langur** *(Presbytis melalophos mitrata)* **L:** 50 cm + **T:** 71 cm, **W:** about 6 kg.
- **3 Yellow-handed Mitered Langur** *(Presbytis melalophos melalophos)* **L:** 50 cm + **T:** 71 cm, **W:** about 6 kg.
- **4 Natuna Island Langur** *(Presbytis natunae)* **L**, **T**, and **W:** no data available.
- **5 Tricolored Langur** *(Presbytis femoralis cruciger)* **L:** 43–61 cm + **T:** 61–83 cm, **W:** 5.8–8 kg.
- **6 Javan Gray Langur** *(Presbytis comata)* **L:** 50–53 cm + **T:** 65 cm, **W:** 6.3–6.6 kg.
- **7 Maroon Langur** *(Presbytis rubicunda)* **L:** 49–57 cm + **T:** 70 cm, **W:** 5.7–6.2 kg.
- **8 Thomas's Langur** *(Presbytis thomasi)* **L:** 55 cm + **T:** 76 cm, **W:** 5–8 kg.

SIMIIFORMES

CATARRHINI

HOMINOIDEA

Hylobatidae

Like the great apes, the gibbons and Siamang that compose the family Hylobatidae lack a tail and tend to hold themselves vertically. As a result, the rib cage is notably well developed. Gibbons and Siamangs live in the upper story of the forest and almost never descend to the ground. Their long limbs are adapted for a particular suspensory form of locomotion known as "brachiation," in which they swing from branch to branch. The phalanges (finger bones) of their hands are markedly elongated, transforming them into veritable hooks that permit them to grasp branches more securely when in full swing. These apes can also hold themselves erect and walk with a bipedal posture, ramrod straight and holding their arms above the head or to the side for balance. They are the only apes that do not construct sleeping nests. They pass the night in a sitting position, hidden by patches of dense foliage. The different species are distinguished particularly by pelage color and by the structure of their songs. However, marked variation in color can exist even within a single species. In some species, the pelage differs between the sexes. For instance, in Capped Gibbons the male is entirely black, whereas the female has silvery fur, with black patches on the head and belly.

Siamang and Gibbons

GENUS *Symphalangus* | **Siamang** | 1 species | Plate 46

Siamangs are the largest members of the Hylobatidae. Males and females have an ebony-colored coat and possess a small tuft of hair, resembling a tail, between the two callosities (hardened skin patches) on the buttocks. Thanks to a large vocal sac, they have a powerful song, more striking than melodious, that carries a long way. The sac, which serves as a resonance chamber, is inflated with air when an individual emits its vocalizations. Whereas the male produces a long, throaty call, the female instead utters barking sounds in response. Siamangs live in lowland or montane forests on Sumatra and the Malay Peninsula, sharing their habitat with Agile and White-handed gibbons (both of genus *Hylobates*).

GENUS *Nomascus* | **Crested gibbons** | 5 species | Plate 46

The different gibbon genera are distinguished particularly by their chromosome numbers: Species of the genus *Nomascus*, like the Siamang, have 52, whereas gibbons in the genus *Hylobates* have 44, and those in the genus *Hoolock* have 38. As is typical for hylobatids, crested gibbons are predominantly herbivorous. They feed on some fifty different plant species, including bamboo shoots, which are abundant in the forests that they inhabit in China, Vietnam, and Laos. Some gibbons may also supplement their diets with insects, such as termites and caterpillars. To drink, these apes dip a hand into a pool of water and then lick off the moisture.

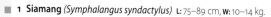

■ **1 Siamang** *(Symphalangus syndactylus)* **L:** 75–89 cm, **W:** 10–14 kg.

■ **2 Yellow-cheeked Gibbon** *(Nomascus gabriellae)* **L:** about 60 cm, **W:** 5.7 kg.

■ **3 Tonkin Black Crested Gibbon** *(Nomascus concolor concolor)* **L:** 45–63 cm, **W:** 4.5–5 kg.

■ **4 Southern White-cheeked Gibbon** *(Nomascus leucogenys siki)* **L:** 45–63 cm, **W:** 5.6–5.8 kg.

■ **5 Northern White-cheeked Gibbon** *(Nomascus leucogenys leucogenys)* **L:** 45–63 cm, **W:** 5.6–5.8 kg.

■ **6 White-cheeked gibbon subspecies not illustrated.**

SIMIIFORMES
CATARRHINI
HOMINOIDEA
Hylobatidae

Gibbons

GENUS *Hoolock* | **Hoolock gibbons** | 2 species | Plate 47

Formerly allocated to the genus *Hylobates*, hoolock gibbons are now classified in the separate genus *Hoolock*. This distinction is based on their number of chromosomes (38, as compared to 44 or 52 in the other genera). Males have a black pelage, whereas females have coppery-colored fur. In both sexes, however, there are two bands of white hair above the eyes. At birth, the infant hoolock gibbon is entirely white; its pelage becomes progressively grayer and eventually black as it grows. In females, the pelage changes in color once again at adulthood.

GENUS *Hylobates* | **Gibbons** | 7 species | Plates 47–49

Gibbons are undoubtedly the most melodious of the apes. Their calls, which comprise an incomparable repertoire, also serve to differentiate species from one another. Gibbons live in monogamous pairs, accompanied by their offspring. Every morning, soon after sunrise, the male and female sing a duet, except for the Mentawai Gibbon and the Silvery Gibbon, which have solo songs. The gibbons' powerful calls have several functions. They are used for territorial defense and also for attracting a mate and strengthening the pair bond. Gibbons form tight-knit families. The female gives birth to a single infant once every three years on average after a gestation lasting six to seven months. As in other apes, infancy is particularly extended in gibbons. The offspring does not become independent until the age of four to five years and may remain with its family for some while thereafter. It is hence common to see a pair with two or even three infants of different ages. It is only at the age of eight to ten years that a maturing gibbon becomes truly adult.

■ 1 **Agile Gibbon** *(Hylobates agilis)* **L:** 42–47 cm, **W:** 5.5–6.4 kg.
■ 2 **Bornean White-bearded Gibbon** *(Hylobates agilis albibarbis)* **L:** 42–47 cm, **W:** 5.5–6.4 kg.
■ 3 **Western Hoolock Gibbon** *(Hoolock hoolock)* **L:** 48 cm, **W:** 6–7 kg.

SIMIIFORMES
CATARRHINI
HOMINOIDEA
Hylobatidae

Gibbons

GENUS *Hylobates* | **Gibbons** | 7 species | Plates 47–49

■ **1 Mentawai Gibbon** *(Hylobates klossii)* **L:** 45 cm, **w:** 5.8 kg.

■ **2 Silvery Gibbon** *(Hylobates moloch)* **L:** 45–64 cm, **w:** 6 kg.

■ **3 Capped Gibbon** *(Hylobates pileatus)* **L:** no data available, **w:** 6–8 kg.

1♂ 2♂ 3♀ 3♂

SIMIIFORMES

CATARRHINI

HOMINOIDEA

Hylobatidae

Gibbons

GENUS   *Hylobates* | **Gibbons** | 7 species | Plates 47–49

■ **1 Müller's Bornean Gibbon** *(Hylobates muelleri)* **L:** 42–47 cm, **W:** 5–6 kg.

■ **2 Malaysian White-handed Gibbon** *(Hylobates lar lar)* **L:** 42–58 cm, **W:** 4.5–7.5 kg.

3 Central White-handed Gibbon *(Hylobates lar entelloides)* **L:** 42–58 cm, **W:** 4.5–7.5 kg.
Subspecies are not indicated on the map.

SIMIIFORMES
CATARRHINI
HOMINOIDEA
Hominidae

In traditional classifications, all great apes (species of the three genera *Gorilla*, *Pan*, and *Pongo*) were allocated to the family Pongidae, while the family Hominidae was reserved for the human genus (*Homo*) and its direct fossil relatives. Now, however, all four genera are included in the Hominidae, which together with the family Hylobatidae constitutes the superfamily Hominoidea. All members of that superfamily are distinguished from other primates by relatively large body size and weight, the lack of a tail, and an increased brain volume.

Orangutans

GENUS *Pongo* | **Orangutans** | 2 species | Plate 50

Orangutans have been geographically isolated for more than ten thousand years, ever since rising sea levels separated Borneo and Sumatra as two distinct islands. Eventually, the Bornean and Sumatran orangutan populations became two completely separate species. *Pongo abelii*, the Sumatran Orangutan, is particularly distinguished by a more oval-shaped face and longer pelage, as well as a bright orange coloration of the fur. By contrast, the Bornean Orangutan, *Pongo pygmaeus*, has a rounder face, shaped like a figure eight in males, and its pelage color varies from orange-red to chocolate brown. There are also specific differences in behavior. In some Sumatran populations, individuals readily move around in small groups, whereas Bornean Orangutans are consistently solitary. It is noteworthy that several orangutan populations in Sumatra and Borneo make and use various kinds of tools, such as twigs serving to prize open the husks of certain fruits. Following the example of "chimpanzee culture," researchers unhesitatingly talk of "orangutan culture."

In orangutans, as in many other primates, males and females show marked morphological differences. Such sexual dimorphism is partly due to the fact that males are almost twice as big as females and possess a fat-filled flange on either side of the face, forming a facial disk. This inflated structure serves to magnify the characteristic territorial long calls emitted by adult males, and it may also play a part in attracting females.

Orangutans are the only strictly arboreal great apes, confining their movements exclusively to trees. Their long forelimbs, elongated hands (with reduced thumbs), and prehensile feet permit them to progress in a special manner: They grasp branches with their feet while their hands take hold of the trunk of a neighboring tree. They are particularly active in the morning and at the end of the afternoon, using branches and leaves to build nests in trees as resting sites during the middle of the day. Orangutans live in different forest types—lowland, moderately montane, or swampy—where they feed on leaves, fruits, bark, and insects.

1 Bornean Orangutan *(Pongo pygmaeus)* L: 78–97 cm, W: 40–50 kg (female); 60–90 kg (male).

2 Sumatran Orangutan *(Pongo abelii)* L: 78–97 cm, W: 40–50 kg (female); 60–90 kg (male).

1♂

2♂

2♀

2♂

2j

LORISIFORMES

LORISOIDEA

Lorisidae

Two families are distinguished within the superfamily Lorisoidea: The Lorisidae of Asia and Africa and the Galagidae, which occur only in Africa. They are small or medium-sized primates that inhabit forests where the vegetation is relatively dense. They are all nocturnal and typically solitary in behavior.

The African lorisids move around slowly and very discreetly along branches without ever leaping. The tail is reduced or completely lacking. During progression, they strongly grasp each support with the hand, in which the second finger is greatly reduced to form a veritable pincer. In the foot, there is marked opposition between the big toe and the other digits. The second toe bears a grooming claw. The muscles of the limbs can remain contracted for prolonged periods without tiring, thanks to a blood-retention system in the musculature that permits continued respiratory exchange.

Angwantibos and Pottos

GENUS *Arctocebus* | **Angwantibos** | 2 species | Plate 51

In angwantibos, as in pottos, the second digit is reduced in the hand, permitting a very firm grasp on small branches, to which angwantibos can cling for long periods without tiring. They can also defend themselves by biting if attacked. Angwantibos move through the trees slowly at moderate heights, where they forage for various kind of animal prey, notably caterpillars, grasshoppers, ants, and beetles.

GENUS *Perodicticus* | **Potto** | 1 species | Plate 51

Pottos are nocturnal and move around stealthily in the dense vegetation of secondary forests, where they can easily conceal themselves. They forage for fruits, exudates, and various small invertebrates, especially ants. When faced with a potential predator, a potto will defend itself by bowing its head between its arms, firmly grasping the supporting branch. In this posture, it will utter loud grunts and inflict bites with its powerful canine teeth. While doing so, it will try to dislodge its attacker by butting with its neck, a veritable shield through which spines of the cervical vertebrae protrude. Pottos are territorial and mark the boundaries of their home ranges with urine and secretions produced by glands located close to the genital organs. Males live in quite extensive territories, ranging in size from twenty-five to almost one hundred acres, overlapping the smaller ranges of one of more females, each no larger than twenty-five acres.

Every year, after a gestation of six and a half months, the female gives birth to one or two infants. Initially, the offspring remain sheltered in a hiding place arranged among the branches. Male pottos can begin to breed at the age of six months and females at eight months.

■ **1 Calabar Angwantibo** *(Arctocebus calabarensis)* **L:** 23–30.5 cm + **T:** 8 cm, **W:** 260–465 g.

■ **2 Golden Angwantibo** *(Arctocebus aureus)* **L:** 24.5 cm + **T:** 1.5 cm, **W:** 210 g.

■ **3 Bosman's Potto** *(Perodicticus potto)* **L:** 30–39 cm + **T:** 3.7–10 cm, **W:** 850 g–1.6 kg.

LORISIFORMES

LORISOIDEA

Galagidae

Bushbabies, all of the family Galagidae, owe their name to calls uttered by one of the largest-bodied species, which resemble the bawling of a human neonate. In addition to big, globular eyes adapted for nocturnal life, they have notably large, mobile ears. They are hence endowed with good hearing, which is vital for detecting the small invertebrates on which they feed, in addition to exudates, fruits, and seeds. Bushbabies move around by running along branches and leaping. They are well adapted for leaping from tree to tree thanks to marked elongation of the hind limbs, which literally function like springs, and a bushy tail that serves for balance. During the daytime, they often sleep in tree hollows. One or two infants are born after four months of gestation. They are then carried around in the mother's mouth for about six weeks before they begin to move around independently in the trees.

Bushbabies

GENUS *Euoticus* | **Needle-clawed bushbabies** | 2 species | Plate 52

Needle-clawed bushbabies, comprising the genus *Euoticus*, owe their common name to the claw-like shape of the nails on both hands and feet. These permit an excellent grip on bark and branches in the crowns of trees in the tropical rain forests where they live. The diet of needle-clawed bushbabies, in addition to insects and fruits, includes a large proportion of saps and other exudates of trees. Exudates are detected by smell and by regularly visiting many trees, sometimes as many as one hundred, while foraging. These bushbabies sleep rolled into a ball in tree forks.

GENUS *Otolemur* | **Thick-tailed bushbabies** | 3 species | Plate 52

These are the biggest of the bushbabies. They are less acrobatic than their smaller-bodied relatives when running and climbing along branches. But they will unhesitatingly leap from one tree to another. Whereas males are mainly solitary, especially when foraging for invertebrates, small birds, lizards, and mammals, females form small groups of a few individuals together with their offspring. Thick-tailed bushbabies share their territories of about twenty-five acres with other bushbaby species.

GENUS *Galago* | **Lesser bushbabies** | 20 species | Plate 52

Lesser bushbabies have dense, silky fur. The extremities of their digits bear expanded pads covered with thick skin that act like suckers, allowing them to grasp smooth branches. While resting, their long ears are folded away toward the back of the head. They live in wooded savannas and sleep in tree holes, where they are protected from predators.

■ 1 **Southern Needle-clawed Bushbaby** *(Euoticus elegantulus)* L: 19 cm + T: 24 cm, W: 270–300 g.

■ 2 **Brown Thick-tailed Bushbaby** *(Otolemur crassicaudatus)* L: 31 cm + T: 42 cm, W: 1.2–1.5 kg.

■ 3 **Allen's Bushbaby** *(Galago alleni)* L: 20 cm + T: 20–24 cm, W: 314 g.

■ 4 **Mohol Bushbaby** *(Galago moholi)* L: 16 cm + T: 23 cm, W: 200 g.

■ 5 **Demidoff's Bushbaby** *(Galago demidoff)* L: 13 cm + T: 18 cm, W: 69–81 g.

SIMIIFORMES

CATARRHINI

CERCOPITHECOIDEA

Cercopithecidae

The family Cercopithecidae is a vast assemblage containing one hundred species in twenty-one genera. They are found in diverse regions of Africa, at the southern end of the Arabian Peninsula, in Southern and Central Asia and in Japan. They are divided into the two subfamilies Cercopithecinae and Colobinae based on dietary grounds.

Cercopithecinae

Cercopithecines are also known as "cheek-pouched monkeys" because they can store a large quantity of food in cheek sacs and then gradually process it over the course of the day. Cercopithecines are diurnal monkeys. They live predominantly in trees, but, in contrast to other primates, they can readily adapt to terrestrial life. In fact, some species, such as baboons, spend most of their time on the ground. They are characterized by a relatively thickset body, with the forelimbs generally shorter than the hind limbs. In the hand, the thumb is well developed. According to species, the tail is variable in length, and it is sometimes reduced or absent. Unlike in several New World monkeys, however, in cercopithecines the tail is never prehensile.

Patas Monkey and Forest Guenons

GENUS *Erythrocebus* | **Patas monkey** | 1 species | Plate 53

Patas Monkeys, which are committed to terrestrial life, hold the world record among primates for running speed, being able to reach thirty-five miles an hour. They live in open habitats, in savannas sparsely dotted with acacia trees. Females, which are half the size of males, lead the group of ten to thirty individuals and defend an extensive territory. Although males are not territorial, they nevertheless serve as sentinels within their groups, warning of approaching predators by violently shaking branches and bushes.

Patas Monkeys travel between 750 yards and almost six miles in a day, depending on the richness of the habitat, in search of food: grasses, leaves, fruits, mushrooms, insects, small vertebrates, and birds' eggs. During the hottest hours of the day, they rest in the shade of big trees, and they spend the night in the safety of the crowns of acacia trees, with each adult occupying a different tree. Although they generally tend to be quite silent, Patas Monkeys bark noisily to sound the alarm or when two groups meet up and fight over the same territory.

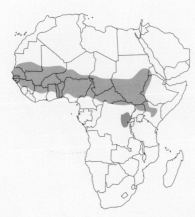

1 Patas Monkey *(Erythrocebus patas)* **L:** 49 cm (female); 60–87 cm (male) + **T:** 49–61 cm, **W:** 4–7 kg (female); 7–13 kg (male).

2 Hamlyn's Owl-faced Guenon *(Cercopithecus hamlyni hamlyni)* **L:** 56 cm + **T:** about 60 cm, **W:** 3.7 kg (female); 5.4 kg (male).

3 Kahuzi Owl-faced Guenon *(Cercopithecus hamlyni kahuziensis)* **L:** 56 cm + **T:** about 60 cm, **W:** 3.7 kg (female); 5.4 kg (male).

SIMIIFORMES
CATARRHINI
CERCOPITHECOIDEA
Cercopithecidae
Cercopithecinae

Forest Guenons

GENUS *Cercopithecus* | **Forest guenons** | 25 species | Plates 53–59

Guenons live in forests and wooded savannas and sometimes inhabit mangroves. They spend most of their time in the crowns of trees, where they feed predominantly on fruits. These monkeys play a major role in seed dispersal and hence in regeneration of the forests where they live. Together with other species, notably birds, they serve as gardeners. Guenons are social monkeys living in groups organized around females, which are closely related to one another because they spend their lives in the group in which they were born. Each species is easily recognizable thanks to different color patterns on the pelage, particularly on the face.

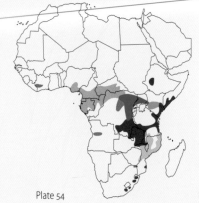
Plate 54

Plate 54

1 **Stairs's White-collared Guenon** *(Cercopithecus albogularis erythrarchus)* **L**, **T**, and **w**: no data available.

2 **Kolb's Guenon** *(Cercopithecus albogularis kolbi)* **L**, **T**, and **w**: no data available.

3 **Blue Monkey** *(Cercopithecus mitis stuhlmanni)* **L**, **T**, and **w**: no data available.

4 **Golden Monkey** *(Cercopithecus kandti)* **L**: 47–56 cm + **T**: 68–75 cm, **w**: 4.2 kg (female); 7.3 kg (male).

4b **Blue Monkey subspecies not illustrated.**

5 **Eastern Spot-nosed Guenon** *(Cercopithecus nictitans nictitans)* **L**, **T**, and **w**: no data available.

6 **Western Spot-nosed Guenon** *(Cercopithecus nictitans martini)* **L**: 43–66 cm + **T**: 50–60 cm, **w**: 4 kg (female); 6.3 kg (male).

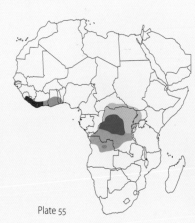
Plate 55

Plate 55

1 **Schmidt's Red-tailed Guenon** *(Cercopithecus ascanius schmidti)* **L**, **T**, and **w**: no data available.

2 **Whiteside's Red-tailed Guenon** *(Cercopithecus ascanius whitesidei)* **L**, **T**, and **w**: no data available.

3 **Black-nosed Red-tailed Guenon** *(Cercopithecus ascanius atrinasus)* **L**: 42–49 cm + **T**: 65–77 cm, **w**: 3.3 kg (female); 4.2 kg (male).

3b **Red-tailed Guenon** subspecies not illustrated.

4 **Buettikofer's Spot-nosed Guenon** *(Cercopithecus petaurista buettikoferi)* **L**, **T**, and **w**: no data available.

5 **Lesser Spot-nosed Guenon** *(Cercopithecus petaurista petaurista)* **L**: 41–49 cm + **T**: 65–71 cm, **w**: 3 kg (female); 3.8 kg (male).

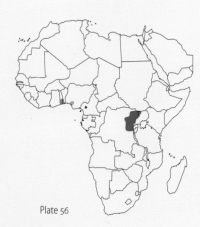
Plate 56

Plate 56

1 **Red-bellied Guenon** *(Cercopithecus erythrogaster erythrogaster)* **L**, **T**, and **w**: no data available.

2 **Nigerian White-throated Guenon** *(Cercopithecus erythrogaster pococki)* **L**: 47 cm + **T**: about 60 cm, **w**: 2.4–2.8 kg.

3 **Sun-tailed Guenon** *(Cercopithecus solatus)* **L**: 50–70 cm + **T**: 60–78 cm, **w**: 4–6 kg (female); 6–9 kg (male).

4 **Preuss's Guenon** *(Cercopithecus preussi)* **L**: 57 cm + **T**: about 60 cm, **w**: up to 10 kg.

5 **L'Hoest's Guenon** *(Cercopithecus lhoesti)* **L**: 47–56 cm + **T**: about 60 cm, **w**: 3.5 kg (female); 5.9 kg (male).

2♂

3

4

5

SIMIIFORMES
CATARRHINI
CERCOPITHECOIDEA
Cercopithecidae
Cercopithecinae

Forest Guenons

GENUS *Cercopithecus* | **Forest guenons** | 25 species | Plates 53–59

Plate 57

1 **Red-tailed Moustached Guenon** *(Cercopithecus cephus cephus)* L: 49–56 cm + T: 69–78 cm, W: 2.9 kg (female); 4.1 kg (male).

2 **Ngotto Moustached Guenon** *(Cercopithecus cephus ngottoensis)* L: 49–56 cm + T: 69–78 cm, W: 2.9 kg (female); 4.1 kg (male).

3 **Red-eared Guenon** *(Cercopithecus erythrotis)* L: 35–40 cm + T: 60–70 cm, W: 4–4.9 kg.

4 **Sclater's Guenon** *(Cercopithecus sclateri)* L: 30–50 cm + T: 50–70 cm, W: 3 kg (female); 4 kg (male).

Plate 58

1 **Crested Mona Monkey** *(Cercopithecus pogonias)* L: 46–53 cm + T: 73–81 cm, W: 3.1 kg (female); 4.5 kg (male).

2 **Wolf's Mona Monkey** *(Cercopithecus wolfi)* L: 48 cm + T: 78 cm, W: 2.7 kg (female); 3.8–4.2 kg (male).

3 **Dent's Mona Monkey** *(Cercopithecus denti)* L: 48 cm + T: 78 cm, W: 2.7 kg (female); 3.8–4.2 kg (male).

4 **Campbell's Mona Monkey** *(Cercopithecus campbelli)* L: 40–50 cm + T: 64–72 cm, W: 2.2 kg (female); 4.3 kg (male).

5 **Mona Monkey** *(Cercopithecus mona)* L: 42–54 cm + T: 58–76 cm, W: about 2.7 kg.

Plate 59

1 **De Brazza's Guenon** *(Cercopithecus neglectus)* L: 46–56 cm + T: 53–69 cm, W: 4.4 kg (female); 7–8 kg (male).

2 **Salongo Guenon** *(Cercopithecus dryas)* L: 35 cm + T: 60–70 cm, W: 2.2 kg (female); 3 kg (male).

3 **Diana Monkey** *(Cercopithecus diana)* L: 44–57 cm + T: 71–86 cm, W: 5–5.4 kg.

4 **Roloway Monkey** *(Cercopithecus roloway)* L: 44–57 cm + T: 71–86 cm, W: 5–5.4 kg.

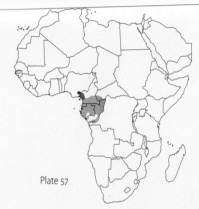

Plate 57

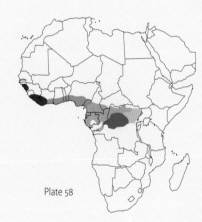

Plate 58

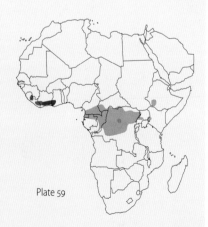

Plate 59

Savanna Guenons

GENUS *Chlorocebus* | **Savanna guenons** | 6 species | Plate 60

Savanna guenons are the most widely distributed primates and the most abundant on the African continent, living in savannas, wooded zones, the semidesert expanses of the Sahel, and in montane regions.

   These guenons are very social, mostly living in relatively large groups. Groups range in size from five to seventy or more individuals, occupying territories about one hundred acres in size. Numerous studies have shown that the vocal repertoire of savanna guenons, containing a score of different call types, includes three clear-cut alarm calls that are emitted in response to particular predators. Each of these calls elicits distinct responses from other members of the group. For instance, on hearing the alarm call signifying "predatory bird," group members scan the sky, whereas they attentively examine the ground in response to "snake predator," and take refuge in the trees when a predatory cat is indicated. Experiments have shown that savanna guenons can recognize every individual in their own groups from vocalizations produced, and that they are also capable of deceptive behavior directed toward conspecifics.

- **1 Green Monkey** *(Chlorocebus sabaeus)* L: 42–49 cm + T: 56–63 cm, W: 3.2–4.5 kg.
- **2 Tantalus Monkey** *(Chlorocebus tantalus)* L: 42–49 cm + T: 56–63 cm, W: 3.2–4.5 kg.
- **3 South African Vervet Monkey** *(Chlorocebus pygerythrus pygerythrus)* L: 42–49 cm + T: 56–63 cm, W: 3.2–4.5 kg
- **4 Bale Mountains Vervet Monkey** *(Chlorocebus djamdjamensis)* L: 42–49 cm + T: 56–63 cm, W: 3.2–4.5 kg
- **5 Kenyan Vervet Monkey** *(Chlorocebus pygerythrus johnstoni)* L: 42–49 cm + T: 56–63 cm, W: 3.2–4.5 kg
- **5b Savanna guenon** species not illustrated.

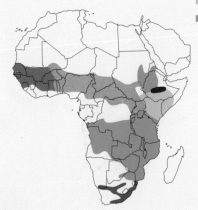

1

2♂

5♂

1♂

3♀ +j

4

SIMIIFORMES

CATARRHINI

CERCOPITHECOIDEA

Cercopithecidae

Cercopithecinae

Swamp Monkey and Talapoins

GENUS *Allenopithecus* | **Swamp monkey** | 1 species | Plate 61

These robust, heavily built, black and green guenons occur only in a small area of swampy primary forest in the Democratic Republic of Congo and Angola. Their partially webbed hands and feet allow them to swim well, a capacity that permits them to escape from predators. They often use their hands to probe around in swampy areas and mud to capture small fish. In addition, their diet includes fruits, roots, and insects. They are particularly attracted to nectar, licking the insides of various flowers. In this way, they contribute to the pollination of certain trees in the forest, as do many bird and bats.

GENUS *Miopithecus* | **Talapoins** | 2 species | Plate 61

Talapoins are the smallest of the Old World monkeys. In body form and pelage color they are quite similar to South American squirrel monkeys. But, despite their small size, they are closely related to other guenons.

Talapoins live in groups of about forty to fifty individuals. They live in primary and secondary forests, never very far from rivers, swampy areas, or mangroves. They are good swimmers. Talapoins are omnivorous, feeding mainly on fruits but also eating leaves, flowers, insects, eggs, and freshwater shrimps. They regularly raid human crops and flooded areas close to human habitations.

■ **1 Gabon Talapoin** *(Miopithecus ogouensis)* **L:** 25 cm + **T:** 52 cm, **W:** 750–820 g (female); 1.25–1.28 kg (male).

■ **2 Angolan Talapoin** *(Miopithecus talapoin)* **L:** 25 cm + **T:** 52 cm, **W:** 750–820 g (female); 1.25–1.28 kg (male).

■ **3 Allen's Swamp Monkey** *(Allenopithecus nigroviridis)* **L:** 45–46 cm + **T:** 50 cm, **W:** 3.7 kg (female); 5.9 kg (male).

INFRAORDER
PARVORDER
SUPERFAMILY
FAMILY
SUBFAMILY

SIMIIFORMES

CATARRHINI

CERCOPITHECOIDEA

Cercopithecidae

Cercopithecinae

White-eyelid Mangabeys

GENUS *Cercocebus* | **White-eyelid mangabeys** | 6 species | Plate 62

White-eyelid mangabeys are generally quite similar to guenons, except that they are slightly bigger and more massive. Like crested mangabeys (*Lophocebus*), they are forest-living monkeys, but generally occupy the undergrowth. They mainly move around and feed on the ground and in the lower levels of the forest, where they find fruits, leaves, and small invertebrates. They are organized into multimale-multifemale groups containing about twenty individuals. When they are sexually receptive, females develop large swellings of red-colored skin in the anogenital region. On average, they give birth to a single infant a year, after a gestation lasting six months. Just a few minutes after birth, the infant mangabey is already able to hold onto the mother's fur.

■ 1 **Collared Mangabey** *(Cercocebus torquatus)* **L:** 60 cm + **T:** 66 cm, **W:** about 10 kg.

■ 2 **Agile Mangabey** *(Cercocebus agilis)* **L:** about 60 cm + **T:** 70 cm, **W:** 4.7 kg (female); 9.2 kg (male).

■ 3 **Sooty Mangabey** *(Cercocebus atys atys)* **L:** about 60 cm + **T:** 70 cm, **W:** 8.5 kg.

■ 4 **White-naped Mangabey** *(Cercocebus atys lunulatus)* **L:** about 60 cm + **T:** 70 cm, **W:** 8.5 kg.

■ 5 **Tana River Mangabey** *(Cercocebus galeritus)* **L:** 48–55 cm + **T:** 57–70 cm, **W:** 10.2 kg.

■ 6 **Golden-bellied Mangabey** *(Cercocebus chrysogaster)* **L:** about 60 cm + **T:** 70 cm, **W:** 4.7 kg (female); 9.2 kg (male).

SIMIIFORMES

CATARRHINI

CERCOPITHECOIDEA

Cercopithecidae

Cercopithecinae

Crested Mangabeys

GENUS *Lophocebus* | **Crested mangabeys** | 3 species | Plate 63

Crested mangabeys are notably distinguished from white-eyelid mangabeys in that they are arboreal, occupying the upper levels of the forest and descending to the ground only very rarely. They live in small groups that do not usually contain more than fifteen individuals but include several males. Crested mangabeys do not defend territorial boundaries, and there may be extensive overlap between the home ranges of several groups. They often associate with other species, such as guenons or colobus monkeys.

■ **1 Black Crested Mangabey** *(Lophocebus aterrimus)* **L:** 53 cm + **T:** 75 cm, **W:** 15 kg (female); 21 kg (male).

■ **2 Osman Hill's Gray-cheeked Mangabey** *(Lophocebus albigena osmani)* **L:** 52–56 cm + **T:** 74–80 cm, **W:** 5.6 kg (female); 7 kg (male).

■ **3 Johnston's Gray-cheeked Mangabey** *(Lophocebus albigena johnstoni)* **L:** 52–56 cm + **T:** 74–80 cm, **W:** 5.6 kg (female); 7 kg (male).

■ **4 Gray-cheeked Mangabey** *(Lophocebus albigena albigena)* **L:** 52–56 cm + **T:** 74–80 cm, **W:** 5.6 kg (female); 7 kg (male).

SIMIIFORMES

CATARRHINI

CERCOPITHECOIDEA

Cercopithecidae

Cercopithecinae

Barbary Macaque

GENUS *Macaca* | **Macaques** | 22 species | Plate 64

The Barbary Macaque is the only species belonging to the genus *Macaca* that occurs in Africa; all others are Asian (Plates 34–37). It lives in the high cedar forests in the Middle and High Atlas mountains of Morocco and Algeria, where it feeds on acorns, cones and needles of conifers, bark, mushrooms, and small invertebrates. In winter, when the entire habitat is covered with snow, these monkeys owe their survival to the cedar trees, which then provide almost all of their food.

1 Barbary Macaque *(Macaca sylvanus)* **L:** 45–60 cm + **T:** almost nonexistent, **W:** about 10 kg (female); 15–17 kg (male).

1♀ +j

1♂

1

1

SIMIIFORMES

CATARRHINI

CERCOPITHECOIDEA

Cercopithecidae

Cercopithecinae

Baboons

GENUS *Papio* | **Baboons** | 5 species | Plates 65 and 66

Baboons are the biggest of the cheek-pouched monkeys. Although they readily climb trees, they move around almost exclusively on the ground. They occupy a range of different habitats: dry tropical forests, savannas, and arid areas, including high plateaus and mountains up to elevations of 15,000 feet.

Baboons have a massive body and a markedly elongated, doglike snout. Males, in particular, have strikingly big canine teeth and are an impressive size, twice as big as females. The canines provide a defensive weapon not only during tense interactions between males when access to females is concerned, but also against predators. Baboons live in large groups, with an average of about fifty individuals but sometimes more than one hundred. In Hamadryas Baboons, social organization has several levels. The basic unit is a harem; that is, a single male accompanied by several females. A cluster of three or four harems is associated with bachelor males to form a clan, and several clans together form a band. In the final level, several bands join together, particularly to share sheltered sites where they spend the night. The overall association is quite fluid, with subgroups separating and then rejoining as the days pass.

The social life of baboons is governed by distinct male and female hierarchies. They otherwise maintain friendly relationships with one another, either between adult males and females or between adults and young individuals. Baboons are omnivorous, with a basic diet of fruits, seeds, roots, and leaves. This is complemented not only by small invertebrates but also antelopes, flamingos, and other mammals and birds, as baboons are effective hunters. They also regularly raid crops. Baboons were considered sacred in ancient Egypt, embodying the god Thoth, deity of scribes and inventor of language and writing.

■ 1 **Chacma Baboon** *(Papio ursinus)* **L:** 59 cm + **T:** 76 cm, **W:** 16.8 kg (female); 20.5 kg (male).

■ 2 **Guinea Baboon** *(Papio papio)* **L:** 69 cm + **T:** 56 cm, **W:** 17.5 kg.

■ 3 **Yellow Baboon** *(Papio cynocephalus)* **L:** 59 cm + **T:** 76 cm, **W:** 16.8 kg (female); 20.5 kg (male).

■ 4 **Olive Baboon** *(Papio anubis)* **L:** 60–74 cm + **T:** 43–50 cm, **W:** 14.5 kg (female); 28 kg (male).

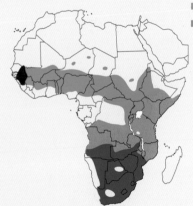

1

2♀ +j

2♂

3

4

Baboons and Gelada

GENUS *Papio* | **Baboons** | 5 species | Plates 65 and 66

GENUS *Theropithecus* | **Gelada baboon** | 1 species | Plate 66

Gelada Baboons inhabit prairie grasslands on the Ethiopian high plateaus, at elevations between 4,500 and at least 12,000 feet. The fur is dense, particularly in males, which have a long cape of hair on the shoulders resembling a mane. These monkeys are herbivorous, and grasses make up more than 90 percent of their diet. The remainder essentially consists of seeds, leaves, bulbs, and insects. They spend a very large part of the day, almost 60 percent, squatting on the prairie, plucking bundles of grass with their hands. In fact, their ischial callosities—reinforced areas of skin beneath the tail that ensure comfort while sitting—are particularly well developed. In other baboon species females signal sexual receptivity by displaying reddened swellings around their genital organs. But Geladas squat continually, so the original "buttock" display has been replaced by a signal on the chest, which is far better adapted and efficient. In both males and females there is an hourglass-shaped patch of hairless skin on the chest. This is bright red in color, and when females become receptive many small vesicles appear around its edges. Geladas live in large bands containing between a few dozen and several hundred individuals, composed of small subgroups or harems. Each harem has a single adult male accompanied by several females, usually three or four but sometimes as many as twenty. Just after awakening, when they leave the cliffs where they have taken shelter for the night, Geladas spend a couple of hours engaged in social activities, notably intense bouts of grooming, which provide a veritable social cement within groups.

■ **1 Hamadryas Baboon** *(Papio hamadryas)* **L:** 75 cm + **T:** 55 cm, **W:** 12 kg (female); 21 kg (male).

■ **2 Gelada Baboon** *(Theropithecus gelada)* **L:** 50–65 cm + **T:** 32–40 cm, **W:** 11.5 kg (female); 20 kg (male).

1♀ + j

1♂

2♂

2♀

1♂

2♂

SIMIIFORMES

CATARRHINI

CERCOPITHECOIDEA

Cercopithecidae

Cercopithecinae

Drill and Mandrill

GENUS *Mandrillus* | **Drill and mandrill** | 2 species | Plate 67

Like members of the genus *Papio*, the forest-living species *Mandrillus leucophaeus* and *Mandrillus sphinx* have long snouts, but their heads are much bulkier, forming a kind of mask. Whereas the Drill's face is uniformly black, apart from the pink-edged lips, the head and hindquarters of the Mandrill are vividly ornamented in blue, red, and yellow. Particularly in males, these colors increase in intensity with increasing rank in the social hierarchy. It is thought that coloration of the buttocks might facilitate coordinated movements of the group through dense vegetation. For, in contrast to other baboons, Drills and Mandrills live in dense tropical rain forest in the western part of the Congo basin, where Nigeria, Cameroon, and Gabon converge. They travel great distances every day, between one and three miles within vast territories between 2,500 and 12,400 acres in area. They feed essentially on fruits and seeds, complemented by bark, leaves, and various invertebrates (mainly insects) and small mammals, birds, and tortoises. There is considerable competition for the place of dominant male at the head of a harem, so spats and fights are frequent and sometimes violent. Both species, and particularly the Drill, count among the most threatened of primates, victims of deforestation and the bushmeat trade.

■ **1 Drill** *(Mandrillus leucophaeus)* L: 66–70 cm + T: 8–12 cm, W: about 10 kg (female); 17 kg (male).

■ **2 Mandrill** *(Mandrillus sphinx)* L: 56–81 cm + T: 7 cm, W: 11.5 kg (female); 27 kg (male).

1 ♂

1 ♀

1 j

2 ♂

2 ♀

SIMIIFORMES

CATARRHINI

CERCOPITHECOIDEA

Cercopithecidae

Colobinae

Leaf monkeys belong to the smaller of the two subfamilies of Old World monkeys, the larger containing the cheek-pouched monkeys. Colobines are gracile animals, with slender bodies and limbs and a long tail, often ending in a tuft, used to maintain balance when leaping from tree to tree. They live in groups of ten to more than one hundred members, including one or several adult males and numerous females accompanied by their offspring. Considerable time is devoted to social relationships, especially grooming bouts that serve to strengthen the bonds between individuals. Leaf monkeys feed almost exclusively on leaves, which are difficult to digest because of their high cellulose content. Like cows, colobine monkeys have a specialized stomach divided into several compartments, some of which house colonies of bacteria adapted for degradation and digestion of the cellulose in leaves. Because this food source is poor in nutrients, very large quantities must be ingested. Fermentation of the leaves generates gas in the stomach, so leaf monkeys often have swollen, distended bellies.

Colobus Monkeys

GENUS *Colobus* | **Black-and-white colobus monkeys** | 5 species | Plate 68

Monkeys of the genus *Colobus* are recognizable from their black-and-white fur, which tends to be shaggy and forms different patterns according to species. Like other leaf monkeys, they possess a compartmentalized stomach, which ensures better digestion of the large quantities of leaves that they consume. They live in groups of about fifteen individuals in both primary and secondary forests as well as in certain wooded montane areas. A newborn colobus monkey is entirely white. These primates have been heavily hunted because their pelage was greatly sought after for making coats.

■ 1 **Ursine Colobus Monkey** *(Colobus vellerosus)* **L:** 61–66 cm + **T:** 75–81 cm, **W:** 8.3–19.9 kg.

■ 2 **Tanzanian Black-and-white Colobus Monkey** *(Colobus angolensis palliatus)* **L:** 53–59 cm + **T:** 70–82 cm, **W:** 7.4 kg (female); 9.6 kg (male).

■ 3 **Black Colobus Monkey** *(Colobus satanas)* **L:** 63–67 cm + **T:** 80 cm, **W:** 11 kg.

▪ 4 **Mount Kenya Colobus Monkey** *(Colobus guereza kikuyuensis)* **L:** 57–61 cm + **T:** 69 cm, **W:** 8–9 kg (female); 13.5 kg (male).

■ 5 **Congo Guereza** *(Colobus guereza occidentalis)* **L:** 57–61 cm + **T:** 69 cm, **W:** 8–9 kg (female); 13.5 kg (male).

■ 6 **Kilimanjaro Guereza** *(Colobus guereza caudatus)* **L:** 57–61 cm + **T:** 69 cm, **W:** 8–9 kg (female); 13.5 kg (male).

■ 7 **King Colobus Monkey** *(Colobus polykomos)* **L:** 60–63 cm + **T:** 87–88 cm, **W:** 8.3–9.9 kg.

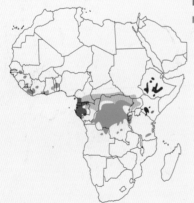

SIMIIFORMES

CATARRHINI

CERCOPITHECOIDEA

Cercopithecidae

Colobinae

Red and Olive Colobus Monkeys

GENUS *Piliocolobus* | **Red colobus monkeys** | 9 species | Plate 69

These colobus monkeys are particularly distinguished by the color of their pelage, which is partially orange-brown. They inhabit different types of forest and are very acrobatic, performing impressive leaps from one tree to another. They sometimes associate with other species to benefit from more effective warnings if one of their predators approaches. For instance, in West Africa red colobus monkeys exploit the sentinel role played by Diana Monkeys (*Cercopithecus diana*). The latter occupy the upper levels of the forest, where they have a particularly good view of the surroundings.

GENUS *Procolobus* | **Olive colobus monkey** | 1 species | Plate 69

The olive-gray pelage color of Van Beneden's Olive Colobus Monkey provides very effective camouflage among branches and tangled lianas, concealing them from their predators, which are mainly chimpanzees, leopards, and raptors. They are social and, like most other colobus monkeys, live in groups of about ten individuals, including several adult males and females. This is the only Old World monkey in which the mother carries her offspring in her mouth.

■ 1 **Van Beneden's Olive Colobus Monkey** (*Procolobus verus*) L: 46.5–48 cm + T: 56–57 cm, W: 4.2–4.7 kg.

■ 2 **Zanzibar Red Colobus Monkey** (*Piliocolobus kirkii*) L: 53–63 cm + T: 60–70 cm, W: 7–10.5 kg.

■ 3 **Central African Red Colobus Monkey** (*Piliocolobus foai oustaleti*) L: 53–57 cm + T: 66.5 cm, W: 8.2 kg.

■ 4 **Pennant's Red Colobus Monkey** (*Piliocolobus pennantii*) L: 53–63 cm + T: 60–70 cm, W: 7–10.5 kg.

■ 5 **Upper Guinea Red Colobus Monkey** (*Piliocolobus badius badius*) L: 53–57 cm + T: 66.5 cm, W: 8.2 kg.

■ 6 **Temminck's Western Red Colobus Monkey** (*Piliocolobus badius temminckii*) L: 53–57 cm + T: 66.5 cm, W: 8.2 kg.

SIMIIFORMES

CATARRHINI

HOMINOIDEA

Hominidae

Traditionally, all great apes (members of the three genera *Pan*, *Pongo*, and *Gorilla*) were allocated to the family Pongidae. The family Hominidae was reserved for the genus *Homo* (humans). Now, however, these four genera are often combined in the Hominidae, which constitutes the ape superfamily Hominoidea along with the Asian gibbons (Hylobatidae). All apes differ from other primates in their large body size, lack of a tail, and large brain volume.

Gorillas

GENUS *Gorilla* | **Gorillas** | 2 species | Plate 70

Behind the brutish aura that has fed myths and film scenarios, the gorilla is a gentle herbivorous giant. Lowland and Mountain gorillas belong to two species, which occupy very different biotopes. Lowland Gorillas inhabit dense equatorial rain forests in the Congo basin, whereas Mountain Gorillas live in montane forests dominated by bamboos and giant lobelias. Both species live in harems containing about ten individuals. Females accompanied by their offspring are dominated by one or sometimes two adult males characterized by pale gray hairs on the back, accounting for the name "silverback." It is the females that migrate on reaching adolescence to join another group and thus avoid inbreeding. The female usually gives birth to one infant once every four years, following a gestation lasting eight and a half months. Although the mothers primarily take care of the offspring, the dominant male also spends much time playing with young individuals in the group and may take care of a small orphan after the mother has disappeared, sharing its nest at night.

With a body weight of 85 kg for females and 170 kg for males, gorillas are the largest extant primates. The particularly impressive silverback struts around while drumming on his chest and will unhesitatingly charge when faced with danger. In contrast to chimpanzees or orangutans, which prefer to sleep high up in trees, gorillas construct nests on the ground every evening.

The diet of gorillas is provided largely by plants, consisting of mainly grasses, giant nettles, lobelias, and bamboos, but also some fruits, along with occasional insects. Until recently, gorillas were considered to be the least intelligent of the great apes, but recent observations have revealed that gorillas can use tools, notably employing sticks to test the water level in swamps before crossing them.

■ **1 Eastern Lowland Gorilla** *(Gorilla beringei graueri)* **L:** 150–170 cm, **W:** 80 kg (female); 170 kg (male).

■ **2 Mountain Gorilla** *(Gorilla beringei beringei)* **L:** 150–170 cm, **W:** 95 kg (female); 160 kg (male).

■ **3 Western Lowland Gorilla** *(Gorilla gorilla)* **L:** 150–170 cm, **W:** 70 kg (female); 170 kg (male).

1♂

2♂

3♀ +j

3j

3♂

Chimpanzee and Bonobo

GENUS *Pan* | **Chimpanzee and bonobo** | 2 species | Plates 71 and 72

The genus *Pan* includes the Common Chimpanzee and the Bonobo. The latter are also misleadingly called pygmy chimpanzees, but they are almost as big as chimpanzees and are simply more slender and gracile.

Like humans, chimpanzees have traditions and cultures. They make and use tools, hunt monkeys smaller than themselves (primarily red colobus monkeys) as well as various mammals, and engage in warfare with neighboring chimpanzee communities. Chimpanzees and Bonobos are social, living in so-called fission-fusion systems. In other words, they separate into small subgroups that go off in different directions to forage for food. As a rule, they meet up again in the evening, close to the trees in which each individual will construct a sleeping nest with leaves and branches. Males spend a considerable amount of time patrolling the boundaries of their group's territory. The hierarchy among males is quite rigid, and complex political strategies are employed to acquire power, often benefiting from alliances with certain influential females.

The discovery of the Bonobo, long thought to be no different from the chimpanzee, was made by the German anatomist Ernst Schwarz. In 1929, while studying the collections of the colonial museum in Tervuren, Belgium, he was intrigued by the presence of a skull that was too small to belong to a chimpanzee. The slender Bonobo is more arboreal than the chimpanzee and is found only in an enclave of flooded tropical forest in the northern region of the Democratic Republic of Congo. With its prominent sideburns and a hairstyle that is almost chic, the Bonobo appears to live by the motto "make love not war." In fact, in this species sex is substituted for violence in the resolution of conflicts and serves as veritable social cement. It is the females that act as leaders and decision-makers in a community containing some thirty individuals or more. Bonobos and chimpanzees are primarily frugivorous but also consume many different plants, honey, mushrooms, and occasionally insects and small vertebrates. In addition, some communities engage in hunting. Both chimpanzees and Bonobos have an extensive vocal repertoire. They also communicate with one another with facial signals, and in the laboratory they have proved capable of learning symbolic languages, such as manual sign language.

■ 1 **Central Chimpanzee** *(Pan troglodytes troglodytes)* L: 82 cm, W: 32–47 kg (female); 40–60 kg (male).

■ 2 **Eastern Chimpanzee** *(Pan troglodytes schweinfurthi)* L: 82 cm, W: 32–47 kg (female); 40–60 kg (male).

■ 3 **Western Chimpanzee** *(Pan troglodytes verus)* L: 82 cm, W: 32–47 kg (female); 40–60 kg (male).

1♀ +j

2♂

3♂

1♂

SIMIIFORMES
CATARRHINI
HOMINOIDEA
Hominidae

Chimpanzee and Bonobo

GENUS *Pan* | **Chimpanzee and bonobo** | 2 species | Plates 71 and 72

1 Bonobo *(Pan paniscus)* L: 70–76 cm, W: 31 kg (female); 39 kg (male).

Background Reading

Cartmill, M., and Smith, F. H. *The Human Lineage*. Wiley-Blackwell, Hoboken, NJ, 2009.

Cheney, D. L., and Seyfarth, R. M. *How Monkeys See the World: Inside the Mind of Another Species*. University of Chicago Press, Chicago, IL, 1992.

De Waal, F. *Our Inner Ape: A Leading Primatologist Explains Why We Are Who We Are*. Riverhead Books, New York, NY, 2006.

De Waal, F., Macedo, S., and Ober, J. *Primates and Philosophers: How Morality Evolved*. Princeton University Press, Princeton, NJ, 2006.

Jolly, A. *Lucy's Legacy: Sex and Intelligence in Human Evolution*. Harvard University Press, Cambridge, MA, 2001.

Kingdon, J. *Kingdon Field Guide to Mammals of Africa*. Academic Press, New York, NY, 2003.

Martin, R. D. *Primate Origins and Evolution: A Phylogenetic Reconstruction*. Princeton University Press, Princeton, NJ, 1990.

Ravosa, M. J., and Dagosto, M. (eds.). *Primate Origins: Adaptations and Evolution*. Springer, New York, NY, 2007.

General Books on Primates

Cachel, S. M. *Primate and Human Evolution*. Cambridge University Press, New York, NY, 2006.

Campbell, C. J., Fuentes, A., MacKinnon, K. C., Bearder, S. K., and Stumpf, R.M. (eds.). *Primates in Perspective*. Oxford University Press, Oxford, UK, 2011.

Conservation International Pocket Identification Guide series: *Marmosets and Tamarins; South Asian Primates; Lemurs of Madagascar: Diurnal and Cathemeral Lemurs; Lemurs of Madagascar: Nocturnal Lemurs; Monkeys of the Atlantic Forest of Eastern Brazil*; etc. Various authors; illustrations by Stephen D. Nash et al. Conservation International, Arlington, VA, 2007–2010.

Dixson, A. F. *Primate Sexuality: Comparative Studies of the Prosimians, Monkeys, Apes, and Human Beings*. Oxford University Press, Oxford, UK, 2012.

Groves, C. *Primate Taxonomy*. Smithsonian Institution Press, Washington, DC, 2001.

Hartwig, W. C. (ed.). *The Primate Fossil Record*. Cambridge University Press, Cambridge, UK, 2002.

Matsuzawa, T. *Primate Origins of Human Cognition and Behavior*. Springer, New York, NY, 2001.

Redmond, I. *The Primate Family Tree*. Firefly Books, Buffalo, NY, 2001.

Rowe, N. *The Pictorial Guide to the Living Primates*. Pogonias Press, East Hampton, NY, 1996.

Strum, S., and Fedigan, L. M. *Primate Encounters: Models of Science, Gender, and Society*. University of Chicago Press, Chicago, IL, 2002.

Lemurs, Lorises, and Tarsiers

Alterman, L., Doyle, G. A., and Izard, M. K. (eds.). *Creatures of the Dark: The Nocturnal Prosimians*. Plenum Press, New York, NY, 1995.

Garbutt, N. *Mammals of Madagascar*. Yale University Press, New Haven, CT, 2007.

Gursky, S., Wright, P. C., and Simons, E. L. (eds.). *Tarsiers: Past, Present, and Future*. Rutgers University Press, New Brunswick, NJ, 2003.

Mittermeier, R. A., Hawkins, F., and Louis, E. E. *Lemurs of Madagascar*. 3rd ed. Conservation International, Arlington, VA, 2010.

Sussman, R. W. *Primate Ecology and Social Structure. Volume 1: Lorises, Lemurs and Tarsiers*. Pearson Custom Publishing, Needham Heights, MA, 2001.

Monkeys

Garber, P. A., Estrada, A., Bicca-Marques, J. C., Heymann, E. W., and Strier, K. B. (eds.). *South American Primates: Comparative Perspectives in the Study of Behavior, Ecology, and Conservation*, Springer, New York, NY, 2008.

Kinzey, W. G. (ed.). *New World Primates: Ecology, Evolution, and Behavior*. Aldine de Gruyter, New York, NY, 1997.

McGraw, W. S., Zuberbühler, K., and Noë, R. *Monkeys of the Taï Forest: An African Primate Community*. Cambridge University Press, Cambridge, UK, 2007.

Ross, C. F., and Kay, R. F. (eds.). *Anthropoid Origins: New Visions*. Kluwer Academic/Plenum Publishers, New York, NY, 2004.

Strum, S. *Almost Human: A Journey into the World of Baboons*. University of Chicago Press, Chicago, IL, 2001.

Sussman, R. W. *Primate Ecology and Social Structure. Volume 2: New World Monkeys*. Pearson Custom Publishing, Needham Heights, MA, 2000.

Whitehead, P. F., and Jolly, C. J. (eds.). *Old World Monkeys*. Cambridge University Press, Cambridge, UK, 2000.

Apes

Caldecott, J., and Miles, L. (eds.). *World Atlas of Great Apes and Their Conservation*. University of California Press, Berkeley, 2005.

De Waal, F., and Lanting, F. *Bonobo: The Forgotten Ape*. University of California Press, Berkeley, 1998.

Fossey, D. *Gorillas in the Mist*. Houghton Mifflin, New York, NY, 1983.

Goodall, J. *The Chimpanzees of Gombe: Patterns of Behavior*. Harvard University Press, Cambridge, MA, 1986.

Goodall, J. *Through a Window: My Thirty Years with the Chimpanzees of Gombe*. Mariner Books, New York, NY, 2010.

Harcourt, A. H., and Stewart, K. J. *Gorilla Society: Conflict, Compromise, and Cooperation Between the Sexes*. University of Chicago Press, Chicago, IL, 2007.

Lappan, S., and Whittaker, D. (eds.). *The Gibbons: New Perspectives on Small Ape Socioecology and Population Biology*. Springer, New York, NY, 1998.

Lindsey, J., and Goodall, J. *The Great Apes*. MetroBooks, New York, NY, 1999.

Morris, D., and Parker, S. *Planet Ape*. Firefly Books, Buffalo, NY, 2009.

Schwartz, J. H. (ed.). *Orang-Utan Biology*. Oxford University Press, New York, NY, 1988.

Van Schaik, C. *Among Orangutans: Red Apes and the Rise of Human Culture*. Belknap Press of Harvard University Press, Cambridge, MA, 2004.

Internet Sites

http://pin.primate.wisc.edu

http://www.primate-sg.org

http://www.primate.org